the First Sunday

SUNDAY ROSE SERIES

Book 1

The First Sunday

A NEW BEGINNING & A NEW LIFE

R. Jay Berry

he First Sunday
Copyright © 2011 by R.Jay Berry. All rights reserved.

No part of this publication may be reproduced, stored in a retrieval system or transmitted in any way by any means, electronic, mechanical, photocopy, recording or otherwise without the prior permission of the author except as provided by USA copyright law.

Scripture quotations marked (KJV) are taken from the *Holy Bible, King James Version*, Cambridge, 1769. Used by permission. All rights reserved.

This novel is a work of fiction. However, several names, descriptions, entities, and incidents included in the story are based on the lives of real people.

The opinions expressed by the author are not necessarily those of Imperium Publishing.

Published by Imperium Publishing
1097 N 400th Rd | Baldwin City, KS 66006 USA
www.imperiumpublishing.com

Cover design by April Marciszewski
Interior design by Christina Hicks

Published in the United States of America

ISBN: 978-1-64318-017-5
1. Fiction / Biographical
2. Fiction / African American / Historical

Dedication

This book is dedicated to my grandmother, Georgia Turner Biggins, who taught me the meaning of family and to stand up for my Christian beliefs even when others do not agree.

To my mother, Litha Gray Stradford, and my father, Jimmie Riley Stradford, who always wanted the best for their children. They told us we could be anything, could go anywhere, and should live life to the fullest, but that we had to put God first.

Thank each of you for the person I am today.

Introduction

This is the story of Sunday Rose Tyler, who departed this world at the age of ninety-two. She lived a good life and was a loving sister, mother, grandmother, great-grandmother, aunt, and matriarch of the Tyler family. There is no doubt she was loved by her family, but some would say it was difficult to always express that love because of her strong-willed nature. Sunday Rose would do anything for her family, but sometimes she went overboard because of that love.

The Tyler family saga begins in Kittman, Texas, a small town approximately eighty-eight miles south of Dallas, Texas. Kittman had a population of 2,573 residents, and most were close and distant relatives. The main attractions for this booming city were church services every first and third Sundays with the church-circuit rotation of ministers.

Usually at the end of church services, there would be dinner on the church grounds under the shade trees for people to congregate. The women would bring their fried chicken, greens, candied yams, and hot water cornbread for dinner. Some of the women had specialty desserts that they liked to bring, like sweet potato pies, fruit pies, and peach cobbler—everybody's favorite. After eating, the men would talk about their crops and what problems they had on their respective farms. Life seemed to be good for all of the residents of Kittman. Amos and Lottie Tyler were a big part of the Kittman community. They were longtime residents of this small town and were well liked by all of their neighbors.

Chapter 1

Our story begins on the windy, cool day of October 19, 1908, at the state fair of Texas. This was the date that Amos Lee Tyler would remember as the day he first saw his bride-to-be, Miss Lottie June Williams. When Amos caught the first glimpse of this young woman, he had a funny feeling in the pit of his stomach. He saw a tall, thin woman with long, satin-black, Indian-grade hair that stopped at the top of her buttocks. Her caramel-colored skin made her hair look even darker as it blew in the wind. He had seen prettier women, but there was something about this one that caught his eye in a different way. Amos watched the way Lottie laughed and moved. It suggested she was sure of herself and could handle any given situation. He made a point of watching Lottie for the rest of that day, and he already knew that by the end of the next week, he would get to know more about the young woman he was sure he intended to marry.

Amos, only twenty years old, had run his own farm since his parents, Edward and Sarah, and younger sister, Rose, had died in a tornado two years before. Amos had been away at the time in the next county buying his first bull at his father's request. After the burial of his parents and sister, Amos swore he would rebuild and make a go of his unforeseen inheritance. He would remember all of his father's teachings and make the farm pay for itself. Just to make ends meet, Amos had to work day in and day out because he did not want to ask for help, but he was determined to do even better than his father. However, by country standards, Amos's father had done quite well on his small spread. Edward had left his son approximately three hundred acres of land with the same number of cattle to tend. He made sure that Amos knew how to run the farm and how to make the land take care of him. On occasion, some of the nearby neighbors came to Amos's father for advice on land or cattle purchases or even how to make their land more profitable. He always helped his neighbors any way he could, and Amos always listened attentively to what his father's advice was and learned these lessons well. Amos was virtually alone now, with no other family members nearby.

The only other relatives Amos had were four cousins in Hobbs, New Mexico, but they were not close. They were his first cousins, but he had not seen any of them in at least ten years. They were the children of his father's brother, who had died from an unknown illness in 1895. His cousins did not come to the funeral services for his parents and sister, but his neighbors helped him with the services, along with his father's words, "I know you will always make the best and right decisions."

Everyone liked Amos, but he had made no close friends in school or at church that could help console him during the loss of his family. Amos was a good student, but he had no intentions of doing anything with his life but what he learned from his father. His mother had often asked him if there were any pretty girls in his class that he liked, but girls were the last thing on his mind. She was afraid her son would never get married because he never seemed happy unless he was working with his father doing some farm-related chore. Amos was not a shy boy, and girls certainly found him attractive because they went out of their way at school and at church to get his attention but to no avail. He knew that when the time was right for him to meet the right woman, the Lord would put her in his path.

Lottie Williams lived with her parents, four brothers, and maternal grandmother. Her parents were considered well off in those days by country standards. Her maternal grandfather, who had passed away three years earlier, had built their house. He'd made sure his family had enough room; he built the house with four bedrooms and a dining room. This was considered somewhat of a mansion—as verbalized by many of the townspeople.

Lottie's father had completed some schooling, but her mother had completed high school, and she made sure all of her children knew the benefits of a good education. It was instilled into all of the Williams children that they would finish high school. The determined Lottie went on to college for two years. Because she was the only girl, she had become a good cook and was able to do most jobs in and out of the field, and she was proud of it.

Lottie was fully aware of what it took to run a farm and take care of a family. But Lottie had often thought of becoming a teacher. She had taught the Sunday school class for the kindergarten-age children at her church for the last three years, and she loved it. The children loved coming to her class because she always made the lessons interesting. Lottie was a free spirit who loved writing poems about nature. She liked the peace and quiet of the country, so she would often steal away to write her poems or prepare her Sunday school lessons in solitude underneath the large pecan tree in the pasture close to her home. Though Lottie had several friends from school and church, she loved being alone to think about her life and what she wanted to do with it. Everyone liked Lottie because she always had a smile on her face and had a good word to say to everyone she met.

After a brief courtship of six months, Amos knew he had made the right decision to marry this young woman, so he did the gentlemanly thing and asked Lottie's father, John, for her hand in marriage. While only nineteen, Lottie was of age, given the times, and was prepared for marriage, thanks to both of her parents. After a long conversation with Amos, Lottie's parents believed Amos to be a good man and told him they expected him to take good care of their only daughter. Amos would never forget this conversation and Lottie's father's words: "All of the decisions that you make for the rest of your life should be made with your family in mind. You will be the head of the household, but your wife will and should be your helpmate in everything." When Amos heard these words, he immediately thought of his parents because that was the type of marriage they had. With tears in his eyes, all he could say was, "Yes, sir, I will remember this."

Amos and Lottie were married in a small family ceremony in late April 1909 at the New Zion Baptist Church. Reverend Jeremiah Potter performed the ceremony on his scheduled monthly church-circuit visit to Kittman, Texas, in the Sunnyvale County church.

Even though Amos knew he had made the right decision and was marrying the perfect woman, he still felt a little sad that his own parents and sister were not in attendance on this important day in his life. His mind kept going back to the last conversation he'd had with his father and his last words to him: "Son, you have made your mother and me so proud of you that I think you're ready to take on more responsibility around the farm. It's time you get your first experience in purchasing the bull for the Tyler hill pasture. Remember what we've talked about as you make your decision and never let anyone rush you in spending your money." Amos's father never saw the purchase education. It was instilled into all of the Williams children that they would finish high school. The determined Lottie went on to college for two years. Because she was the only girl, she had become a good cook and was able to do most jobs in and out of the field, and she was proud of it.

Lottie was fully aware of what it took to run a farm and take care of a family. But Lottie had often thought of becoming a teacher. She had taught the Sunday school class for the kindergarten-age children at her church for the last three years, and she loved it. The children loved coming to her class because she always made the lessons interesting. Lottie was a free spirit who loved writing poems about nature. She liked the peace and quiet of the country, so she would often steal away to write her poems or prepare her Sunday school lessons in solitude underneath the large pecan tree in the pasture close to her home. Though Lottie had several friends from school and church, she loved being alone to think about her life and what she wanted to do with it. Everyone liked Lottie because she always had a smile on her face and had a good word to say to everyone she met.

After a brief courtship of six months, Amos knew he had made the right decision to marry this young woman, so he did the gentlemanly thing and asked Lottie's father, John, for her hand in marriage. While only nineteen, Lottie was of age, given the times, and was prepared for marriage, thanks to both of her parents. After a long conversation with Amos, Lottie's parents believed Amos to be a good man and told him they expected him to take good care of their only daughter. Amos would never forget this conversation and Lottie's father's words: "All of the decisions that you make for the rest of your life should be made with your family in mind. You will be the head of the household, but your wife will and should be your helpmate in everything." When Amos heard these words, he immediately thought of his parents because that was the type of marriage they had. With tears in his eyes, all he could say was, "Yes, sir, I will remember this."

Amos and Lottie were married in a small family ceremony in late April 1909 at the New Zion Baptist Church. Reverend Jeremiah Potter performed the ceremony on his scheduled monthly church-circuit visit to Kittman, Texas, in the Sunnyvale County church.

Even though Amos knew he had made the right decision and was marrying the perfect woman, he still felt a little sad that his own parents and sister were not in attendance on this important day in his life. His mind kept going back to the last conversation he'd had with his father and his last words to him: "Son, you have made your mother and me so proud of you that I think you're ready to take on more responsibility around the farm. It's time you get your first experience in purchasing the bull for the Tyler hill pasture. Remember what we've talked about as you make your decision and never let anyone rush you in spending your money." Amos's father never saw the purchase that his son made that day, but his words stayed with Amos for the rest of his life.

As the happy couple said their I dos, all Amos could think was that he was very happy marrying Lottie and that he was sure his parents would have loved her as much as he did. After a brief reception at the church, the newlyweds said their good-byes and started their new life at the small farm that would see his family expand and bring him the joy he had seen there with his parents and sister.

Chapter 2

It was now a cool day in September 1928, and Amos Tyler was in the fields feeding his livestock as well as doing his other regular chores with his crops. This daily ritual began each day at 4:00 a.m. and for the most part was completed in about eight hours, unless there were any unforeseen farm-related troubles. Amos was used to the early-morning work hours at the farm. He had not completed his senior year in high school, but he'd gained more education working with his father than being in a schoolroom. He was so glad that he had spent those years with his father, getting to know him and learning what was important—family. Amos had to feed and clothe his family, and his farm was the only source of income, so he did not mind doing his job as a father, husband, and provider for his family.

In the last twenty years, the Tyler family had increased by five children who were as different as night and day. The three boys and two girls were total joy for Amos and Lottie. Their children were all born two years apart. Lottie became pregnant with their first child, Jimmie Lee, in January, about nine months after their wedding, and he was born in 1910. She knew the moment of conception. Needless to say, Jimmie Lee was her favorite. Then there was Sunday Rose, born in 1912; Daniel Ray, born in 1914; Samuel Curtis, born in 1916; and the baby and only other girl, Sarah Louise, born in 1918. Lottie had also given birth to a fourth son in 1916, Edward Eugene. Edward was the younger brother of Samuel Curtis by seven minutes; however, he died shortly after birth. Because medical treatment for African Americans was virtually nonexistent in 1916, the only medical assistance that Lottie had with all of her children was her trusted friend and midwife, Miss Addie. Miss Addie could only guess that Edward had breathing problems. No one ever questioned Miss Addie's diagnosis because she'd helped deliver so many healthy babies.

With Jimmie Lee, now one month shy of his nineteenth birthday, Lottie had had the easiest pregnancy and birth of all of her children with a five-hour delivery. Amos loved his first son. He knew Jimmie would turn out to be a good man and provider. Of all of his three sons, Jimmie was most like him in business matters regarding the farm and the love of the land. He was slow to anger and very knowledgeable about the Tyler acreage and livestock. Jimmie Lee was a handsome young man who looked like a younger version of his father. He was about six feet, two inches tall with big, broad shoulders and big, brown eyes. All of the girls knew that he was a good catch, but his mind was on the running of the family farm. Amos saw a lot of himself in his oldest son.

A New Beginning and a New Life

The delivery of the second Tyler child and oldest girl, Sunday Rose, was the total opposite. Lottie went into labor on a Friday morning, and her daughter was not born until late evening on Sunday. Addie noted she had never seen such a difficult delivery in all of her years of being a midwife. Lottie knew this child's name had to commemorate her birth into the world. Hence, they chose the name Sunday because of her birth on the first holy day in February and Rose because she was the apple of her father's eye and also in honor of his sister, Rose. At her father's request, everyone in the family called her Rose. She was amenable to this decision, but everyone else had to call her by her full given name.

Sunday Rose was self-reliant and spoke her mind. She would be seventeen in five months and in her mind would be grown up in every sense. She was considered by her family and most of the neighbors as a very beautiful young woman. Though only five feet, two inches in height, she had her mother's same caramel complexion with thick and long jet-black wavy hair that came midway down her back. Because she felt like her long hair made her look taller, she wore it down, draped over her left shoulder, most times. Sunday Rose had a nice figure with shapely legs that most of the townsmen liked to look at whenever they saw her.

For as long as Sunday Rose and her family could remember, she had wanted to become a singer. She did not think about going to college to learn another trade, getting married anytime soon, or even getting formal singing training because these things would hold her back from fulfilling her dream. Though not the oldest child, she definitely took charge in most family issues regarding her younger siblings.

Fifteen-year-old Daniel Ray was a true country boy. He was almost six feet tall with freckles that matched the color of his sandy red hair. He had a contagious laugh that his family loved to hear because it would always tend to ease the most difficult family disagreements. This second son was a muscular boy who liked to show his physique as often as possible by not wearing a shirt. Daniel Ray loved to ride horses and work the land. He was definitely going to be a ladies' man, but he also liked to tinker with fixing the farm equipment when it didn't work, which seemed to be more and more often. He would tell his friends all the time, "A good-looking woman and a good horse are all you need." The only dreams Daniel Ray had were riding horses and raising cattle after graduation.

Thirteen-year-old Samuel Curtis had decided to be the professional in the family. Unlike his older brothers, Samuel Curtis took his looks mostly from his mother's side of the family. He was going to be an average height young man with a dimple in his chin that he was proud of. Like his mother, he too had jet-black wavy and curly hair that all of the young girls liked to touch. He was already planning for his graduation in four years and had already made plans to go to college. While he had not decided on a major, he was sure it would have something to do with business. Of all of his brothers, Samuel listened to his mother the most about the value of a good education. While he never got the chance to get to know his younger brother, he often thought what life would be like with two professional Tyler men in the family. They could possibly run the entire town.

Sarah Louise was almost eleven and was a quiet girl who liked to read. She had always been a sickly child who had bouts of croup, pneumonia, and a bad case of scarlet fever that left her with a slightly paralyzed left leg that caused her to have a slight limp. Because she was in the house most of the time recovering from whatever illness she had at the time, Lottie made sure she, along with Sunday Rose, knew how to cook, sew, and take care of the household. She liked to cook the family dinners each night. She loved the planning and preparation of the cooking process. Lottie was proud of her daughter because she was most like her.

Sarah Louise did not have her sister's same good looks or her long, wavy hair, but the two sisters were going to be about the same height. She was always referred to as the cute and shy Tyler sister. Though she spent most of her childhood in bed trying to get over whatever illness she had at the time, she was soft-spoken and always had a smile on her face even when she was ill. She was contented to just stay at home and learn from her mother. How different could two sisters be than the Tyler girls?

Of all of the Tyler siblings, the two oldest children were the closest. Sunday Rose wanted to be like her big brother, so she learned to climb trees, fish, ride horses, and shoot. She loved wearing her beautifully sewn dresses made by her mother and sister to church or any other occasion, but she just loved being around and doing the things her older brother liked to do. Also, the three older siblings had been blessed with beautiful singing voices and often sang at church functions. Sunday Rose was the only Tyler child who aspired to sing in other non-church-related venues, but her parents were totally against this. She knew she had the voice to someday become a great singer, and that was her dream.

The Tyler sisters and brothers truly loved each other, and Sunday Rose made sure that her siblings knew they could come to her with any problem. She had a temper when provoked but would do anything for any of her family members. Amos and Lottie were happy they had a close-knit family.

Chapter 3

Kittman was a small town where everyone knew everybody's business, though Amos and his family minded their own business. He did not believe in gossip or talking about the problems that were associated with farm life. The closest neighbor to the Tyler spread was five miles away. The Johnson farm consisted of Earl Johnson, his wife, Maude, and their twelve children. The two oldest Johnson children, Seth and Bernice, were the same ages as Jimmie Lee and Sunday Rose. This family had ties in the county, as did many of the families that lived there, and were probably the closest friends that Amos and Lottie had.

Because it was expected that country people would marry country people, everyone, including Amos and Lottie, believed Lottie's two oldest children would marry Bernice and Seth. Jimmie Lee was very fond of Bernice, and marrying her was not out of the realm of possibility, but Sunday Rose had no intentions of marrying Seth and settling down into the country life. She had every intention of pursuing a singing career. She even tried to talk her brothers Jimmie Lee and Daniel Ray into a singing career.

The boys were only interested in singing at the church functions if they had to sing. They could not see making it their life's work. Sunday Rose knew given a little time, she could talk her brothers into seeing things her way.

"Do you understand the amount of money we could make by simply singing in a few juke joints here and there?" she would say over and over as she tried to get her brothers to see her way of thinking.

Jimmie Lee was always the voice of reason, and he would say, "Do you realize there are no places in Kittman or probably Dallas that will hire three unknown African Americans to sing in their establishments?"

Sunday Rose had no response to her brother's reality check, but she would not give up. All of her siblings knew that she would not be satisfied just living in Kittman and becoming a wife to a farmer. Sunday Rose thought Seth was somewhat good looking, but he and the country life were boring and uneventful. She wanted more in her life than baking bread, selling quilts at the state fair, or canning food for the winter. Her mind was made up to eventually get married one day, but she was sure that would be well after she was established in her singing career. Also, unlike most young country girls, she never talked much about having children, but she knew she only wanted one child, and that would definitely be a girl. How she knew this fact amazed all of her family.

Chapter 4

Life on the Tyler farm was not without its problems. In July 1909, lightning struck the Tyler barn, and it burned to the ground. Farm equipment, two horses, and a season of hay for the livestock were lost. Of course there were no available funds to rebuild or replenish, but with the help of neighbors and Lottie's father, Amos was able to build a better barn and purchase used equipment.

There was a tremendous drought after the birth of their third child in 1914, and life was very difficult with the loss of the crops. Lottie was well aware of how to survive on the farm when times were tough. She always canned tons of food when the crops were plentiful. Her family may have had smaller portions, but they did not go hungry.

Daniel Ray loved the rodeo and everything associated with it. However, his parents were always afraid he would get hurt because he was careless about his safety. He had fallen from horses on two different occasions with no long-term injuries, but Daniel Ray thought it was funny his parents were so angry.

So it was no wonder that when the annual rodeo circuit came to Kittman in late August 1927, Daniel Ray entered the bronco bull competition, against his parents' wishes. He was tall for his age, so of course he had lied about his age and told the officials he had his parents' approval. Not only did Daniel Ray not complete the required eight-minute bull ride, but after the fall, he had broken both legs. It took him three months to heal completely; then he had to endure the punishment from his father, which was Amos's cup of tea. Amos believed in more than just explaining his point and his expectations to his children; if explaining failed, he had no problem with showing them.

And then there was Sunday Rose and her singing aspirations. Her parents were not in favor of her choice of careers, but that did not stop her from trying to prove to them that she had what it took to have a successful singing career. Her only attempts at singing had been at church services whenever she got the opportunity. On these occasions, the applause and amens from the church members made her think she had what it took to become a successful singer in other venues. She knew if only she was given the appropriate opportunity she would show her family she was going to be a success. She was also a trusting soul who always believed what she was told. Her parents were most perplexed about their daughter because she was so different than any of her siblings. While she would do anything for her brothers and sisters, she could not see herself being her mother or even her younger sister, Sarah.

Lottie and Amos worried about their two girls the most, the oldest girl because of her wandering spirit and her need to be anywhere but close to her family, and the youngest girl because she was always ill and her illnesses seemed to leave her weaker and weaker. She was so frail. Lottie was a praying woman, and she always looked to the Lord for her family problems and guidance on raising her children. She would always end her nightly prayers with, "Lord, please be with my children and guide their footsteps and decisions."

Chapter 5

Given her love of singing and need to be grown and prove she was grown, it was no surprise when Sunday Rose made the decision to leave home in August 1929 three months after graduation from high school at the age of seventeen. Although she was young in age, her determination and drive gave her that added wisdom of anyone in their twenties or older. While Sunday Rose had never been outside of Kittman, she had always talked about going and living in Dallas. So when she made the decision to move to Dallas, she had not thought of where she would live or where she would look for work to earn her keep. These trivial matters did not deserve too much thought. She knew things would work out the minute she stepped off of the bus in Dallas. "I have decided this is what I want to do, and it will not do you any good to try and talk me out of this," she told her parents. They discussed her decision to leave their family, and they decided if they tried to stop her, she would simply run away and they may never hear from her again. Lottie and Amos prayed the night before Sunday Rose left and put her safety in the hands of the Lord.

Sunday Rose hated to leave her family, especially her best friend and older brother, Jimmie Lee, but she had to pursue her dream. "I will be fine, and you don't need to worry about me," she said to her parents the night before leaving.

Her mother felt a sinking feeling that she couldn't explain, but her advice to her daughter was simple. "Trust in the Lord with all thine heart and lean not unto thine own understanding. In all thy ways acknowledge him and he shall direct thy paths." Lottie made sure her daughter had her Bible packed in her suitcase as well as some emergency money safely tucked away in Psalm 91. This was the family's favorite verse and one they each read morning and night before the start and end of their respective days.

Deep down in her heart Lottie knew Sunday Rose would not succeed as a singer and she hoped that the decisions she would make would not have devastating results. Her daughter had a nice enough voice for Sunday services, but Lottie was sure she did not have what it took to be any other type of successful singer because she had no formal training or discipline and wanted neither. Lottie decided to have faith and leave it in the Lord's hands.

At the bus station, her family waited with her. They all sat in silence, not knowing what to say. Amos held back tears because his baby girl was leaving home. "You know your daddy will miss you, and you can always come back home any time," he told her. Unable to speak, she simply hugged her father while the tears flowed freely.

Her good-byes to her other brothers and sister were more than she had bargained for, especially when Jimmie Lee whispered to her, "I love you, Rosie." He was the only one that could call her Rosie. Needless to say, Sunday Rose was glad when the bus arrived. Too many more good-byes and she may not have been able to leave.

This bus ride is where the story begins for Sunday Rose Tyler.

Chapter 6

While on the bus, Sunday Rose sat next to an elderly woman who took the opportunity to grill her about her life in Kittman, her family, and why she was going to Dallas. She learned that the woman's name was Nollie Mae Turner, but she insisted Sunday Rose call her Mama Mae. When Sunday Rose explained that her full name was Sunday Rose Tyler but her family liked to call her Rose, Mama Mae quickly answered, "I'll call you Rose too 'cause you reminds me of a sweet, innocent flower."

"Where you gonna stay while you in the city?" Mama Mae asked Rose. She told her she would find a room for rent somewhere close to the bus station for the time being. Mama Mae firmly commented, "That jus' won't do. You comin' with me to my house. I got a extra room, and I would like the company. I won't take no fer an answer." Rose could only agree and hope that she made her first right decision.

"Yes, ma'am, just until I start working and can afford my own place," she replied.

Mama simply grunted and said, "We'll see."

The First Sunday

When the bus pulled into the depot in Dallas, Rose was happy yet a little nervous. She noticed life in the big city seemed what she looked forward to. Hundreds of people milled around the waiting area and boarded and exited various buses. She noticed that African Americans were a minority in the bus depot. She quickly felt the different treatment from the white people her brother had talked about so often. The majority of the people in Kittman were African American. Rose was now feeling uncomfortable. As she quickly surveyed the first glimpse of her new city, she did not feel at ease in these surroundings. What amazed her was how the white people were getting what she thought was preferential treatment in service, such as help getting off of the bus or helping them to find transportation outside and the African Americans were being ignored or stared at suspiciously. This was her first true taste of being treated differently. She noticed that Mama Mae did not comment or act surprised, so maybe this was normal treatment in the big city.

Mama told Rose they would walk home since she didn't live that far away. On the walk home, she told Rose about her husband, who had passed on a few years before, and their six children, three girls and three boys. They'd all moved from Dallas many years before to different cities, and they all had their own families. She had ten grandchildren, but she had not seen them in several years. As Mama talked, Rose realized how lonely she truly was and that maybe they needed each other. She was sure her mother would approve of Mama Mae, and she thought of the verse her mother had told her the night before she'd left home. The Lord had directed her path and led her to Mama Mae.

As Rose and Mama walked down the various streets on the way to Mama's house, she noticed the neighborhoods and the people that lived there. The homes were small and basically all looked the same. Rose heard greetings from men, women, and children who were genuinely glad to see Mama. The farther they walked, the poorer the neighborhoods seemed to get. They stopped at a small convenience store, where Mama received another greeting from the owner, Joe Gray. "How you been, Mama? What can I git for you?"

"I'm gonna fix a special dinner tonight for my new houseguest, Rose. Rose is from Kittman. She jus' arrived today. Rose, this is Joe. He and his son, Joe Jr., own this here store." Rose smiled and spoke to Joe. Mama paid for the groceries, and she and Rose left the store.

Two blocks later, Mama stopped at a small house that needed painting and that had planks that needed to be replaced on the porch. Rose thought about her home in Kittman and how her mother always made sure their home was clean and maintained. She realized now she may have taken things for granted. Mama unlocked the door, and as they stepped inside, Rose saw four small rooms. There was a stench of mildew that crept in her nostrils, and she thought of mothballs. Rose was grateful to Mama Mae for offering what little she had, and it made her think Mama truly needed her. She was welcomed inside and told to make herself at home. Not sure where to go, Rose sat her bag on the floor and just stood in place. Mama went into the kitchen and put her bags down.

She immediately opened some windows and the back door to air the house. In the bright sunlight, Rose could see that Mama's house was small but very clean. Not a dish was out of place in the kitchen, the beds were made, and everything had its place. There were homemade doilies on the tables and on the back of the divan.

"I know it ain't much, but it's mine. They call this here part of town White Rock. That's funny to me 'cause ain't no whites livin' in White Rock." Mama smiled. "You can sleep in this room and unpack your clothes in this drawer. I will get you some water to wash up, and then I'll begin our dinner. You might think 'bout writin' your folks. I'm sure they is worried 'bout you."

"Yes, ma'am. Thank you, I will." When Rose got a close look at her new room and its furnishings, she noticed a small wrought-iron bed that was rusted and needed painting and an old pedal sewing machine in the corner covered with dust. Rose could tell by seeing the doilies on the couch in the living room that Mama Mae had made them as well as the bedspread on her new bed. There was also a small three-drawer dresser with an oval-shaped swivel mirror. The walls were covered with faded wallpaper, but she could tell the designs were supposed to be yellow flowers. She couldn't help thinking that this was not the room she shared with her sister in Kittman, with its morning sun and pictures on the wall of her family. This was now her new, unassuming room, with no light or family pictures, but she was grateful.

The smells from the kitchen filled the small house, but it reminded Rose of her mother's and sister's meals at home. She had to admit she was hungry. Mama began to sing as she cooked, and this made Rose think she was happy to have someone to cook for again.

Rose was at home, and she was excited the Lord had led her to Mama Mae. She wrote her family and told them about her first day in Dallas. After a wonderful dinner, Rose got ready for bed and couldn't wait to get on her knees and read Psalm 91. She found the money her mother put in her Bible and got teary-eyed. She knew at this moment she had to thank the Lord out loud for all of the blessings he had bestowed upon her this day.

"Lord, please hear your servant's prayer this night. You know what is in my heart and mind. As I ask for your continued protection, please know that I thank you for your grace and mercy. Thank you for sending Mama Mae to watch over me, and I ask that you continue to bless my family in Kittman." Rose then began to read her nightly Bible verse out loud with a different fervor and understanding, and she truly understood now what this verse meant to her mother and why this verse was a Tyler family verse.

> He who dwells in the secret place of the most High shall abide under the shadow of the Almighty.

I will say of the Lord, He is my refuge and my fortress: my God; in him will I trust.

Surely he shall deliver thee from the snare of the fowler, and from the noisome pestilence.

He shall cover thee with his feathers, and under his wings shalt thou trust: his truth shall be thy shield and buckler.

Thou shalt not be afraid for the terror by night; nor for the arrow that flieth by day;

Nor for the pestilence that walketh in darkness; nor for the destruction that wasteth at noonday.

A thousand may fall at thy side, and ten thousand at thy right hand; but it shall not come nigh thee.

Only with thine eyes shalt thou behold and see the reward of the wicked.

Because thou hast made the Lord, which is my refuge, even the most High, thy habitation;

There shall no evil befall thee, neither shall any plague come nigh thy dwelling.

For he shall give his angels charge over thee, to keep thee in all thy ways.

They shall bear thee up in their hands, lest thou dash thy foot against a stone.

Thou shalt tread upon the lion and adder: the young lion and the dragon shalt thou trample under feet.

A New Beginning and a New Life

> Because he hath set his love upon me, therefore will I deliver him: I will set him on high, because he hath known my name.
>
> He shall call upon me, and I will answer him: I will be with him in trouble; I will deliver him, and honour him.
>
> With long life will I satisfy him, and shew him my salvation.
>
> —Psalm 91

She slept well on her first night, but her dreams, oddly enough, were about her family in Kittman. She would begin the next day in fulfilling her dream—or so she thought.

Chapter 7

The light coming from the living room window woke Rose the next morning, and she could smell the aroma of ham, grits, eggs, and biscuits. She heard Mama in the kitchen humming "Pass Me Not, Oh Gentle Savior." She got dressed and washed up, and when she went into the kitchen, breakfast was prepared and on the table. Rose was famished, and after saying grace, she ate to her heart's content. "I likes to see young people eat," Mama commented. Rose ate, and Mama talked about her children, her neighbors, and the neighborhood.

Then the question Rose was expecting to hear came next. "Are you gon' look fer a job in Dallas?"

After swallowing her last bite of grits, Rose responded by saying, "Yes, ma'am. I'm going to be a singer."

Mama did not show any facial expressions or concern, but she did ask, "Where you gonna work until you start singing?"

"I don't know," Rose answered.

Mama was quick to say singing was something that took time. "You gotta' have somethin' to live off of until you start singin.' I knows a lady, a nice white lady, who needs a girl for some cleanin.' I used to work for her long time ago, and she's good people. I can take you over there today to meet her."

Rose was speechless. She had not come to Dallas to clean houses. She did not like to do that at home, but her mother made sure she knew how to properly clean a house.

All she could say was, "Thank you."

An hour or so later, Mama and Rose were walking down the street to the bus stop. They passed Joe's store, and his son, Joe Jr., was out front sweeping. Mama stopped to look at the produce out front and introduce him to Rose. He spoke to Mama and stopped sweeping to stare at Rose. It seemed he was mesmerized by her beauty. Mama explained that Rose would be staying with her for a while and that she might be coming to the store from time to time. Rose was somewhat attracted to this young man. She noticed his muscles and broad shoulders protruding underneath his short-sleeved shirt, his large, light brown eyes, and his small mustache. His smile and stare were intoxicating, and Rose could barely catch her breath with the thought of holding a conversation with him. He was about the height of her brother Jimmie Lee. The only other man that she even spoke to—not related to her in Kittman—was her neighbor, Seth, and she never felt or noticed these things when she was around him. After Mama stopped speaking, Rose and Joe Jr. said their hellos.

"We got to git to the bus," said Mama. Rose and Joe Jr. both wanted to get to know each other a little better, but Rose said good-bye to her first acquaintance in Dallas besides Mama.

Chapter 8

One hour later, Mama and Rose were on a street with large, beautiful houses unlike anything Rose had ever seen. Most of the homes were two- or three-story Victorian homes with wrought-iron fences. One house in particular caught her eye. It was a three-story, white house with yellow trim and a southern-style porch that wrapped around the entire house. The landscape showed off a neatly manicured yard with yellow tulips in flowerbeds on both sides of the porch and also surrounding two large maple trees. Hanging baskets with purple azaleas adorned both the front porch and window boxes under four large picture windows. Rose had never seen anything so beautiful, and she thought to herself, *I can live in a house like this.*

As they came directly in front of the house, Mama stopped in front of the white picket fence gate, and Rose noticed a small placard that said, "Welcome, The Goldsteins."

"We's here. I worked for Ms. Goldstein for twenty-five years, and she is good people. She is fair."

"What did you do for her?" Rose asked.

"I cleaned and cooked sometimes."

Rose had a perplexed look on her face. Surely Mama had something else in mind for her to do. They walked through the gate, and as they walked up the steps to the front door, Mama smiled at a woman she saw through the door.

"Lord, look who's here. What in the worl' done brought you way down here?" the woman said.

"Hello, Flossie. You sho' do look good for a old lady." Both ladies smiled and hugged each other. "I's here to see Ms. Goldstein. This here young woman needs a job, and I tol' her 'bout when I used to work here."

"Good to hear that, Mae, 'cause I cain't make these here stairs the way I used to."

"You got everthin' lookin' so good, Flossie."

"Thank you, girl. I tries. Let me tell Ms. Goldstein you's here."

Rose looked at the furnishings in the house, and she was speechless. She had never seen anything so beautiful. The colors on the inside mirrored the outside. The furniture was all antique white with accents of yellow and purple. There was a baby grand piano with various pictures sitting on top. The pictures displayed a family that had grown up in this house and appeared very happy.

A few moments later, a white-haired woman about four feet, eleven inches in height walked into the room. She had on a bright red dress with a string of pearls and earrings to match. "Hello, Mae. It's good to see you," said Mrs. Goldstein as she grabbed and squeezed Mae's hand. "Who is the beautiful young girl?"

"Hello, Mrs. Goldstein. It's good to see you too. This here is Sunday Rose. I call her Rose 'cause she reminds me of one of your prize roses out back. Rose needs a job, Mrs. Goldstein, and I told her I thought you needed some help. Flossie said the upstairs is gettin' to be too much for her. Rose is from Kittman, and she's stayin' with me fer a spell. I told her you was good people, Mrs. Goldstein." "I see," said Mrs. Goldstein. "Rose, tell me about yourself."

Rose began, "I'm seventeen years old, and like Mama Mae said, I am from Kittman, Texas. My parents have a farm down there, and I am the second oldest child of five children. I have three brothers and one sister. I graduated from high school this year, and I came to Dallas to become a singer. I met Mama Mae on the bus from Kittman, and she was nice enough to let me stay with her until I could earn some money and get my own room."

"Well, Rose, Flossie does need some help with the upstairs. How do you feel about helping Flossie keep the house maintained every day?"

"Ma'am, my mother is a very good housekeeper, and she made sure my sister, Sarah, and I could clean, cook, and sew."

"I see," Mrs. Goldstein remarked. "The job pays fifteen dollars a week. You can eat your lunch in the kitchen and enjoy whatever cook has prepared. I do expect promptness every day, Monday through Friday. There will be some Saturday work serving my guests if we have a dinner party. You will receive an additional ten dollars for this extra work. It is just myself and

Judge Goldstein residing in the house, so you will not need to clean every room upstairs every day, but the judge's sitting room and study will need to be cleaned every day. Every Monday, you will help Flossie clean all of the rugs as well as the windows. She can explain that to you. You will not be required to cook, but on occasion you may have to accompany cook to the market. Your work hours will be from eight to five each day, promptly, and lunch from twelve to twelve thirty. As Mae said earlier, I try to be as fair as I can be, so if there is an emergency or you are not feeling well, I will not deduct your pay for that if all of your chores have been completed. However, I will not tolerate slothfulness or tardiness. I will only bring these issues to your attention on two separate occasions. The third incident will result in your dismissal. Keep in mind, as Mae can attest to, I am very approachable and understanding. Do you think you can abide by the work schedule and the rules?"

"Yes, Mrs. Goldstein," Rose responded.

"Rose, I must tell you, I trust what Mae says, and she is telling me I should trust and hire you. Can I trust you, Rose?"

"Mrs. Goldstein, you can trust me, and I will do a good job. Please give me a chance."

"Very well, you are hired. You can start tomorrow. Flossie will show you where the uniforms are kept, and you will change when you arrive and before you leave each day. Payday is at the end of the day each Friday. You will meet the judge in the morning, and Flossie will answer any questions you may have. If you do not have any questions, I have a lunch to attend. Mae, it was good to see you again, and thank you for thinking of Flossie needing some assistance."

"Mrs. Goldstein, I wus glad to help you out, and it was good seeing you too," remarked Mae. Rose quickly thanked her new employer before she left. While she'd had no intention of cleaning anyone's home as a job, she was happy to be making her own money, and all this had happened her second day in Dallas.

Flossie and Mae showed Rose the rest of the house and what she would be doing beginning in the morning. She also met the cook, whose name was Mabel. She was a cordial woman who seemed glad Rose was joining the Goldstein household. "There is enough lunch if you two would like to stay," Mabel commented. Mae agreed, and Rose was able to hear about the times Mama worked for the Goldsteins.

It was now sinking in to Rose that she had a job. She would be making her own living and at some point would be able to get her own place and take care of herself. A smile appeared on her face. She was on her way to fulfilling her dream.

Chapter 9

When lunch was over, Rose and Mama headed back to the bus stop. Mama was showing Rose which buses to take to get to work each day and how much money she would need to ride every day. Rose should have paid closer attention on the way to her new employer. Mama was so kind to her, and she couldn't help thinking how the Lord had guided her steps and how he was looking out for her. When they arrived back in Mama's neighborhood, on the walk home, Rose caught a glimpse of Joe Jr. helping a customer in his father's store.

Rose told Mama that she would cook dinner for her that night to show her appreciation for all she had done for her. "Mama, you go on ahead, and I will meet you at home. I need to buy some items at the store." This quick visit would allow Rose the opportunity to speak to Joe Jr. alone. When he saw her come into the store, he gazed at Rose with a smile on his face.

"Hello, Ms. Rose. How are you?"

"Hello, Mr. Joe Jr. I am fine. I would like to purchase some items for dinner. I am cooking tonight for Mama."

"What do you know about cooking, Miss Rose?"

"I'll have you know, Mr. Joe Jr., that I am a very good cook and housekeeper."

"Call me JJ; everybody does."

"I will need some fresh green beans, two ears of corn, a fryer, two green tomatoes, and some blackberries."

"This sounds pretty good. Do you need another guest for dinner?"

"No, not tonight. This dinner is just for Mama. I want to show her how happy I am to have met her and that she came into my life. You will be invited to another dinner real soon, Mr. JJ, I am sure. How much is my bill?"

"Let's jus' say you can pay me with dinner."

"How are you able to give away food? What kind of businessperson are you?"

"A very good one. When will you invite me to dinner?"

"I will talk to Mama and let you know. Good-bye and thank you."

"No thanks is needed, Miss Rose."

As Rose walked to Mama's house, she thought of her family and how she missed them. She could see her mother in the kitchen with her sister, Sarah, preparing dinner for the family. Her father and older brother would be coming in from the fields, and her two younger brothers would be doing their chores in the barn before dinner. She would write them a long letter and explain her day and her new responsibilities.

Rose became more teary-eyed as she prepared dinner. She had not realized how attached she was to her family by the everyday chores she was not that interested in doing. She could hear Mama humming a hymn, and it made her remember that in three days it would be the first Sunday and Reverend Potter would be at New Zion to deliver his biweekly sermon. Rose always liked the services on first Sundays because Reverend Potter would ask her two brothers and herself to sing for the congregation. She looked forward to these requests because it made her think she was that much closer to becoming a singer. This was the only time she got to sing in public, and everyone at church told them they liked the way they sang. Rose would make sure she led all of the songs they sang, and her brothers did not care. Mama had already told her about her church, and Rose was looking forward to going with her, although she was not sure about joining a new church yet. This was a big step for her.

As Mama and Rose sat down to fried chicken, green beans, corn on the cob, fried green tomatoes, hot water cornbread, and blackberry cobbler, Rose thought she should say grace; she felt very blessed. Mama told Rose the dinner was very good and how appreciative she was that Rose thought enough of her to spend her money and time taking care of her. They ate and enjoyed each other's company. Rose told Mama about her life on the Tyler farm, and Mama told Rose about her life working at the Goldsteins.'

It had been a long day, and Rose knew she needed to get to bed. She could not be late for work, and she did not need to be tired on her first day. She wished Mama a good night, prepared herself for bed, said her prayers, and read Psalm 91 before closing her eyes.

Chapter 10

Surprisingly, Rose did not sleep very well on her second night. When she did sleep, she dreamt about her job and what she would be doing. She was up at 5:00 a.m. to cook breakfast for her and Mama and get ready in time to leave for the bus stop. She left home at seven, and by seven fifty she was at the back door of Mrs. Goldstein's house, ready to begin her first day of work. Flossie and Mabel were glad to see her. Flossie showed her where to change, and by 8:00 a.m., Rose was upstairs beginning her daily work routine.

At eight thirty, Judge Goldstein walked out into the hallway, and he promptly introduced himself to Rose. "Hello, Rose. It is nice to meet you. I am Judge Goldstein. I heard from my wife that you were joining our employment." Rose noticed that he was about five feet tall, but she assumed in his earlier years he was taller. He walked slightly slumped over but briskly. His nicely combed white hair made him look distinguished, she thought. She imagined what he looked like when he was in court with his black robe against his white hair.

"Yes, sir. It is nice to meet you."
"Have a nice day."
"Yes, sir. I will; thank you."

Rose did not see Mrs. Goldstein until later that morning. According to Flossie, Mrs. Goldstein usually did not come downstairs until close to the lunch hour. She always took her breakfast in bed around nine thirty. She spoke to Rose on her way downstairs.

Rose went about her day, cleaning the master bedroom and restrooms as well as the judge's study. She dusted all five additional bedrooms upstairs even though she did not have to do that but every other week. She wanted to make a good impression.

It was soon lunch time, and Flossie came to get her around noon so they could eat and rest. Mabel had heated up last night's roast with potatoes and carrots. There was also some pound cake for dessert. After lunch, Flossie showed her how to clean the downstairs rugs as well as the windows. While working, Flossie talked to her about the Goldsteins and their life.

"First," she said, "the Goldsteins had four boys, but that middle one died in the war. His name was Aaron. Mrs. Goldstein had whats they called a breakdown when he died. She went away for a while, and no one talked about it. She never talks about the oldest boy either. His name is Louis. He is a lawyer and lives in Chicago. He ain't married yet, but he been seein' this woman for eight years. Edwin, the second son, is a doctor, and he lives in Austin. He and his wife, Julie, has three girls. The baby boy, Joshua, is a teacher, and he and his wife, Millie, ain't got no children yet.

"The Goldstein children don't come to visit their parents very often. After Mrs. Goldstein had her breakdown, she stop tendin' to her other children, and they had to take care of each other. The judge didn't pay 'em no mind either, so they had no mother or father. Louis was the mother and father for his brothers. Mae helped them as much as she could, so they are closer to her than either of their parents. When Mrs. Goldstein came home from the hospital, Mae nursed her jus' like she nursed her children when they were sick. It was really bad 'round here fer a long time."

Rose could never imagine this being her family. Her parents, especially her mother, always made sure her children were well and happy.

"Thanks, Flossie, for telling me about the Goldsteins."

Rose finished her first day and headed back to Mama's house. She'd had a good first day. Mama wanted to hear about her day, and Rose was happy to tell her. After dinner, she said her prayers and thanked the Lord. She read her nightly scripture, Psalm 91, and as soon as her head hit the pillow, she was asleep.

Chapter 11

It had been almost two months since Rose had come to Dallas, met Mama Mae, and got her first job working at the Goldsteins.' While Rose had experienced some great things since she'd left home, her mother had written to her with news from the Tyler family. It seemed her oldest brother and best friend, Jimmie, had gotten engaged to his longtime neighbor and girlfriend, Bernice. For the time being, they were saving money until Jimmie had enough to buy the small Garrett spread ten miles away. Old man Garrett had died five years before, and his wife and children decided to sell the farm. It had one hundred acres, and Jimmie had plans for every acre.

The only other news from home was that Sarah had been sick again, and she had missed two weeks of school. She always had to catch up with her studies after one of her episodes. No news about her two youngest brothers, so she took that to mean they were doing fine. Her mother often told her how she was missed and wondered when they would see her. Her father was working hard as usual, and her mother was making her a quilt.

Rose told her family about her job and what she did every day at work and how she was saving money. She did not mention anything about singing, and her mother never questioned her about it in her letters. Although she had not forgotten about her singing career, it seemed as though it had taken a backseat to her time getting to know her new city and JJ. She also never told her family about JJ and how interested she was in him.

Though they saw each other most every day as she went to work and came home, JJ made sure that Rose was his personal customer whenever she or Mama needed something from the store. JJ had been invited to dinner at Mama's at least once a week and always after church on Sundays, and Mama always made sure she went to bed early on these nights. On the nights and Sundays JJ was invited to dinner, he made sure he brought some food items from his father's store to show his appreciation, and Rose was happy to prepare whatever he brought. Rose and JJ had also gone to JJ's church on two occasions, and she really liked it. There had been long walks on nice evenings, and Rose loved spending these times with JJ. While Rose was getting closer to JJ each day, the only other people she called friends were the ones she worked with each day, and she was fine with that.

Rose often spoke of Mama Mae in her letters and the bits and pieces about her life that she told Rose at varied times. It seemed that her husband had left her after the birth of her last child, and Mrs. Goldstein had helped her a great deal. Mae repaid the favor to her when she became ill. Over the next fifteen years, Mama never heard from her husband until one day she had gotten word that he had died trying to rob a store. She did not tell her children because she was not sure what to say.

Mama often got mail from all of her children, and they all wanted her to come and live with them. It was evident from what Mama told her that all of her children loved their mother and wanted to be close to her. Mae was a very independent woman, but Rose could tell she was depending more and more on her. In some instances, it was like she was the daughter taking care of her mother. Mama did tell her she was thinking about visiting her oldest child sometime soon, but she was not sure. "I do miss my young'uns and my grand-young'uns," she would say. Rose would often see her looking at pictures of her children, grandchildren, and even her husband. Once, Rose had come home from work, and Mama had been asleep in her chair with pictures on the floor. She had been reading a letter from one of her children, and Rose could tell Mama had been crying. In the last few weeks, Rose could sense Mama was seriously thinking about maybe moving to live with one of her children. She knew the time would come, but Rose did not want to think about that if she did not have to.

Chapter 12

Rose was on her way to work one cool day in October when she spotted JJ standing outside of his father's store. He was not working that early in the morning, so why was he there? "What are you doing here so early?" Rose asked him.

"I was waiting for you. What about going out tonight? We could go to dinner. There is this food place run by a friend of my father. Since you have cooked for me, now I would like to repay you. Can I come and get you at seven tonight?"

"You waited out here this early in the morning to ask me to dinner?"

"Yes, I wanted to make sure you did not make any plans."

"Dinner will be good. See you at seven tonight," Rose answered.

As she proceeded on her way to work, she couldn't help thinking how glad she was to see JJ this morning. Rose had actually become quite fond of him. JJ had made a point of always tending to her when she came to the store. She felt very special. "That boy is sweet on you, Rose," Mama would often say. Rose never took the time to think about what Mama said, but she often daydreamed of herself married to JJ.

Rose had a good day at work. She was very good at doing her job. On one occasion, she heard Flossie tell Mabel that she was a "Godsend." The money was also good, and Mrs. Goldstein and the judge treated her better than she'd expected. While she was happy, she still thought about singing. She knew she could not quit her job to fulfill her dreams, but that nagging thought just stayed with her. It was not the money that she aspired to make or the fame she knew she would have. She just loved to sing. Mama asked her to sing at her church several times, but Rose declined. During her frequent daydreams, thoughts of the last time she and her brothers had sung at New Zion brought a smile to her face. The choir director had asked her to sing a solo once, and she was so happy to oblige.

It seemed like the work day would never end. Rose kept looking at the clock, and the hands seemed as though they had stopped. Finally, at five o'clock she left the Goldsteins' house and headed back to Mama's. She had already decided what she was going to wear. Her mother had made her a peach-colored dress with a lace collar and hem and embroidered her initials on each sleeve. This was a special occasion dress that she usually wore to church services, and this was indeed a special occasion.

It was no surprise that JJ was early and arrived to pick Rose up at six thirty. Mama was more than happy to entertain him until Rose finished dressing. "How's your father, Joe? He is the nicest man."

All JJ could manage to say was, "Thank you."

"I am ready," Rose said as she entered the room.

JJ stood and, with a big smile, replied, "Yes, you are. You look great." Mama also commented on what a nice couple they made, and she told them to have a good evening.

JJ asked Rose if she minded riding the bus. He told her where they were going was only a few blocks away. Rose did not mind. They talked about their respective families during their ride. When they arrived at the restaurant, Rose was pleasantly surprised at what she saw. A tall, thin woman with salt and pepper hair greeted them at the door and gave JJ a hug. It was evident she was glad to see him. "Rose, this is Lena, and this is her restaurant," JJ said. Rose glanced at the various people already seated and having dinner, and she thought to herself that this could be a restaurant in Kittman. Everyone she saw looked like people she had seen every day in Kittman. She felt comfortable here.

"Hello, Rose, and welcome to Lady Lena's," she said as she smiled and hugged Rose.

"Hello, it is nice to meet you, Lena."

"I have your table all ready. JJ made sure everything was just right. He came in last week to make sure. Follow me." Lena led them to a table in the corner, and there were a dozen red roses on the table. Rose was so surprised she was speechless. "Your waiter will be Renard, and he will be right over. Enjoy yourselves."

"Lena said you came by last week to make sure everything was just right. You just asked me this morning to go to dinner with you. Why would you make plans last week if you just asked me today? And when did you buy these beautiful roses?" asked Rose.

JJ took Rose's hand and began to explain. "Rose, the first time I saw you two months ago, I knew I wanted you to be my wife. I hoped that we could get to know each other and you would feel the same way about me. I think about you all the time and wonder what you are doing. I see how you care about Mama Mae. I have never met another woman like you. You are so sure of yourself, and I love you with all my heart. I was just hoping you would say yes, so I made these reservations last week and ordered the flowers to be delivered earlier today."

Rose was not sure what to say. She knew she really liked JJ and possibly loved him, and she believed he truly loved her.

"JJ, I do not know what to say. I think I also knew the first time I saw you that you were the one for me, but I wasn't sure. I think I love you too. I can't believe I just said that. JJ, what does this mean?"

"I am hoping it means that you will marry me."

"Marry you. You want me to marry you?"

"I had hoped this evening would turn into a proposal, just not this early in our date. I think I have lost my appetite now. Yes, Rose. I love you. Will you marry me?" JJ reached into his pocket and pulled out a small box. He handed it to Rose, and she opened it. Inside she saw a gold wedding band. "Rose, I know this is not a diamond ring, but I promise you if you say yes, I will get you that diamond engagement ring because you need to know how much I truly love you."

While there was no diamond engagement ring, she wasn't expecting any kind of ring. Again, she was speechless. She looked into JJ's eyes, and she could see the sincerity in his whole face. She knew she loved him, but this was not a part of her plan. Several questions came to her mind. What would her family say? What about her singing career? Would she continue working? Would JJ want children right away? Where would they live? How soon would he want to get married? The last question really was the most important one. Did she really want to marry JJ or anyone right now?

"JJ, I do not know what to say. I have so many questions that I do not know how to respond to."

"I tell you what," said JJ. "Let's have dinner first, and then we can talk on the way home. You order whatever you want." JJ called the waiter over, and they ordered.

Rose could not think about what she was eating, only the list of questions in her head. JJ tried to make small talk, but after that, small talk was not working. They finished their catfish dinners, but neither of them could focus on dessert, so JJ paid the check, hugged Lena, thanked her for a lovely dinner, and they left the restaurant.

Chapter 13

As they walked outside, Rose asked if they could walk home, and JJ agreed. They had walked two blocks in silence when JJ asked, "What are you thinking?"

"I have so many questions I do not know where to start," responded Rose.

"I tell you what, Rose. Let me say what's on my mind first, and if you still have questions, we will address those questions. Is that okay with you?"

"Yes, that is fine," Rose answered, grateful that JJ wanted to start this difficult conversation.

"I am twenty-four years old, and I am the baby of six children. I was in the army for two years, and when I got out, I started helping my father in the store. My mother died five years ago, and my father nearly lost his mind. He had been married to my mother for forty years, and she was his world. Even though he has still not gotten over my mother's death, he can function now. My older brothers did not care about the business, so it was up to me to help him there. My three sisters have their own lives, and they weren't interested in the store, so I am it.

"I have basically not let myself think about my own life because I have been so concerned about my father. But when I saw you, I felt something that I had never felt. I have talked to my father about you, and he thinks you are a good woman and would be a good wife. I am seven years older than you, but you seem so much older than you are. I can see many questions on your face, so let me tell you how I feel about marriage and see if I can answer most of your questions.

"First, I am not looking for a slave or a housekeeper. I am looking for a partner that I can share my innermost thoughts with and that will feel the same about me. I do know you work, and if you want to continue working, that is your choice. I am not going to tell you that I do not want a wife that cooks and tends to our home, but I will share in these chores. Because I do love children, I would like to start a family someday, but not a house full of children. I know I have not met your family, and I would like to do that and ask them for your hand. I am an old-fashioned guy in that respect.

"Since we have not talked about any of this, I am only talking about the way I think. If you say yes, we do not have to get married right away. There would not have to be a large ceremony, but it must be in a church. Whatever we do, we must always put the Lord first. My mother made sure that we all knew the Lord and thanked him daily. Now that I have done most of the talking, what do you think?"

"Wow," said Rose. "You are right. You have said a lot, and you have answered most of my questions. I guess I never thought about marriage right now because we have never talked about it, and I am just now hearing about things I never knew, like about you and your family.

"I can tell you that I came to Dallas to become a singer, not get married right now. That has always been my dream, and I never saw marriage in my near future. My mother always says that the Lord will direct my path, and I was sure he brought me to Dallas to become a singer. My mother also tells us that the Lord may have different plans for us that we can't see. Mama Mae sort of said the same thing.

"I am the second of five children, and while I can cook, as you know, and keep house, I never wanted to do that in Kittman. I now see that maybe the Lord saw me doing these things in Dallas with you. I have no idea what my parents would say, but I am sure they would learn to love you as I do."

JJ smiled, and at that moment, he kissed Rose for the first time. Rose could only think that she'd never felt that way about Seth, and maybe her feelings about marriage were because she did not love him. JJ kissed her again, and this time it was more passionate and longer than the first one. Rose felt a burning inside that she could not describe, but she liked it.

"Does this mean your answer is yes?" JJ asked.

Rose paused for a few seconds and looked JJ in his eyes. "Yes, my answer is yes."

"When can we go and see your family, Rose?"

"Well, let's go on my birthday in February. I was planning to go home anyway. I would like to write them first and let them know about you and when we are coming home. I will not tell them the news, but I want to write them first. I do want to talk to Mama Mae. She really likes you. One thing I think my parents will ask is that we get married in Kittman at our family church. Is that okay?"

"Wherever we get married does not matter, just as long as we get married. The next question is, when do you want to get married?" asked JJ.

"I am not sure. Let me talk to my family first."

The couple held hands and walked the final two blocks to Mama Mae's house. They stood out front talking another thirty minutes. Knowing she had to get up in the morning, Rose told JJ she had to go inside. He kissed her again, and this was even better than the last two. "I will see you tomorrow. I love you," JJ whispered to her.

"I love you too," said Rose.

Chapter 14

Rose could hardly believe that one week ago JJ had asked her to marry him. She had written her family to let them know that she would be home in February and she was bringing someone for them to meet. She wasn't sure what her parents would say, one because of her age, and two because she had not known JJ very long. But she knew Jimmie Lee would be happy for her.

Mama Mae told her she'd known this was going to happen. She kept repeating, "I knowed it, I knowed it all along. It's about time." Rose caught herself humming at work, daydreaming on her ride to and from work, and wishing time would speed up so she could see JJ again. If this was how people in love acted, then she hoped the feeling remained forever. Flossie and Mabel were so happy for her, and even Mrs. Goldstein told her to let her know when she was getting married so she could buy them a proper wedding gift.

There was no set date yet because she wanted to speak to her family first, but she was thinking of an early summer wedding. Summer in Kittman was beautiful, with the blooming of the wildflowers around the church and the adjacent acreage surrounding the church on both sides. She was so glad that JJ did not mind getting married in Kittman. They had not made too many plans, but she did want to know where they would live.

When she arrived at Mama Mae's after work, JJ was in the house waiting for her, as he had done for the last week. He greeted her, gave her a kiss and a long hug, and softly whispered, "I missed you today."

Rose replied, "I missed you too. Are you hungry? I thought I would prepare dinner for you tonight."

"If you do not mind, I would like for you to come and meet my brothers and sisters tonight. My father told them about you, and they all want to meet you."

"Sure, that is fine. Let me tell Mama and make sure she has something to eat. Then I will change and be right with you."

Rose was a little nervous to meet JJ's family, but if they were anything like him, she would love them too. She already liked his father. When JJ told him about their engagement, he said, "JJ has good taste. I am happy to git another daughter." He gave her a big hug and kiss.

Rose could not decide what to wear because she wanted to make a good impression. Mama told her, "Honey, it don't matter. He ain't gonna see what you's wearing anyhow."

Rose decided on a dress her sister had made her for her graduation. JJ looked at her as if she were wearing an evening gown with the smile and gaze he gave her when she came out.

"I will not be late, Mama," Rose said.

"You all sho do make a good couple," Mama responded.

"Rose, just think, soon we will be man and wife."

"I know. I can't wait either. Do you think your family will like me?"

"Rose, they will love you just as much as I do; trust me."

Rose could not help but think that her life had taken a turn that she had not expected, but she knew the Lord was in charge of her life. She knew her mother would say that.

Chapter 15

On the trip to meet JJ's family, Rose asked him where they would live. JJ thought for a second before answering and asked her, "Where would you like to live?"

"I only want somewhere that is close to a bus line so I can get to work and check on Mama. It would be nice if a church were close by."

"Is that all?"

Rose was a little perplexed at his comment and was not sure what he meant. She waited to hear him explain his statement further, but he said nothing else at that moment. As they walked slowly to his father's house, Rose noticed JJ was thinking about something, but he said nothing.

When they arrived at his father's house, everyone was at the door to greet her. She felt very welcomed and loved already. "Everyone, this is your future in-law, Rose," JJ said. He proceeded to introduce his brothers and sisters to Rose. Not one of them hesitated in giving her a hug and kiss and welcoming her to the Gray family. She could not have asked for a nicer family to marry into. They talked at dinner, and she found out all of their names and the respective husbands or wives of those who were married. JJ's father told Rose childhood stories about all of his children and especially JJ. She saw pictures of JJ's mother with her family, and she could see how beautiful she had been. JJ was still very quiet, but she did not ask him any questions.

The night seemed to go by quickly, and before she knew it, it was time to go. Rose got the same hugs and kisses when she was leaving as she had gotten when she had arrived. On the walk home, JJ asked Rose if he could show her something. They walked a few blocks down the road, and they stopped in front of a small, well-kept house with fresh paint, large picture windows with flower boxes and green awnings, a large sitting porch with a swing, a white picket fence, and flower beds that circled the entire house. Rose thought, *What a beautiful little house.*

"This was the house my father bought my mother after they got married. As the family grew, the house got too small, and we moved to the house you saw tonight. My parents gave this house to me. My older brothers did not want it, so what you see is where I grew up and the little handiwork that I have done in the last couple of years, like the paint, the porch, and the flower boxes under the windows. I am not a full-fledged carpenter, but I am pretty handy around the house. So this is where I live now. If you do not mind, this is the house I thought would be perfect for us. It is not very large, but as our family grows, we can build other rooms. It is not the fanciest house, but I have tried to keep it nice. There is a church on the next block, and the bus line is across the street. I have so many good memories in this house with my family. My mother made this a good home, and all of her children were healthy and happy here. What do you think?"

"JJ, I am speechless. I would consider it an honor to live in this house with you and raise our children here," Rose responded.

"JJ, I must confess something to you. I came to Dallas not looking for a husband or even a Mama Mae; I came looking for a singing career. No one person in my family believed singing was what I should do, but it has always been what I wanted to do. Back in Kittman, my two brothers and I sang at church functions, and it became something I loved to do more and more but something my brothers did not. I have never sung anywhere but church, but I feel so happy when I sing. While it might sound strange, I thought I was headed for a great singing career. I had no idea how to get started, and now I am beginning to believe that the Lord had another path for me.

"It started with meeting Mama Mae on the bus ride to Dallas and her offering me a place to live all in the same day, finding a job, meeting you and your family, and now having a house to call my own. My mother always says the Lord works in mysterious ways. I never quite knew what she meant by it, but she would always say it when something happened in our lives that could not be explained. The joy I felt when singing in our church I feel now just being here with you. Now I believe that my singing should be to glorify the Lord. Now that you have heard my confession, what do you think?"

"Nothing more than I knew you were special when I laid eyes on you. Mama Mae saw the same thing as I did too. I feel so blessed to have met you and to know that you are going to spend the rest of your life with me. There is one more thing. I am by no means a rich man, but one thing my family will do is give our share to the Lord. That is what my parents taught us, and that is what I have grown to believe."

"JJ, that is exactly what my parents taught my family. You know, in the country we did not have much money either, but my father always made sure whatever crops or cows he sold at market, the Lord got his share. My mother did not have a job, but she would always carve out whatever monies were the Lord's she made at selling quilts or selling canned food. I think I have met my perfect husband, JJ."

JJ could not hold back any longer, and he kissed Rose in front of their new home. The future Mr. and Mrs. Joe Gray had just started their lives together.

Chapter 16

For the next two months, Rose and JJ were inseparable. They saw each other at the beginning of every day as Rose was on her way to work, on her way back home, at dinner each night, and at church on Sundays with Mama Mae or JJ's father. They shared their first Thanksgiving together as a couple, and Rose loved the idea of cooking dinner for JJ in their future home. Mama Mae and JJ's father were her first dinner guests. There was so much to be thankful for, and she made sure she confessed her thankfulness to the Lord each day when she arose and each night before she went to bed.

For Christmas, Mama Mae went to Houston to visit her children and grandchildren. She was so happy to see her family again. She left Rose in charge of the house. She trusted Rose as though she were one of her own.

Rose helped prepare Christmas dinner with JJ's sisters at her future father-in-law's house. The whole family was there, and it made Rose think about her family and all of the love she'd witnessed and received. She could not wait for the Grays to finally meet the Tylers.

JJ's father gave the grace before dinner, and he made a special point of saying thank you to the Lord for sending Rose to his son and his family. That made Rose feel even more welcomed, and she held back a tear in her left eye.

There was a lot of good conversation during dinner about the upcoming nuptials. JJ and Rose explained that it would be a small ceremony at her family church in Kittman, and her sister would be her maid of honor. JJ had already asked his oldest brother to be his best man. Rose asked her new sisters-in-law if they would help her send out wedding invitations and make the wedding cake. They all seemed thrilled at Rose's requests and for thinking enough of them to include them in her special day. She already knew that her mother and Sarah would want to make her wedding dress, so she was not worried about that.

After dinner, Rose helped clean up the kitchen. Soon after, family members began to leave. JJ's father excused himself from their company. The two of them were now left alone. JJ was happy that now he could finally give Rose her Christmas present in private. As they sat on the couch talking about the events of the day, JJ expressed his love for her again and told her how lucky he was to have her in his life. "You know there is nothing I won't do for you if it is in my power," he said.

"I do know that, and the same goes for me."

"I was not sure what to give you for Christmas. I wanted it to be something that was from my heart and that you would like. Merry Christmas, my sweet Rose."

A New Beginning and a New Life

As Rose began to open the small box, her heart rate started to speed up with anticipation. When she got to the actual small box, she slowly opened it and saw a gold heart necklace. "There is an inscription on the back," JJ added.

As Rose turned the heart over, she read out loud, "'Our love is forever.' Oh, JJ, this is beautiful. I have never had anything like this before. Thank you so much." She gently kissed him on the lips.

"You are welcome. Do you like it?"

"Yes, very much. Please help me put it on. I will never take it off. Now for your gift. I could not bring it here, so we have to go back to our new home."

"You did not have to give me anything. When I look at you, I see my Thanksgiving, Christmas, New Year's, and every other holiday there is right now."

"You are so sweet, but I did buy you something because I love you and you are the best man," Rose told him. With that they headed to their new home-to-be, and as JJ opened the front door, he saw a large box in the middle of the floor with a big, red bow around it. "I spoke to your father a few weeks ago about this, and he helped me with what's inside."

JJ smiled and took the wrapping paper off. To his amazement, it was a box of assorted tools. JJ had told Rose that he was a handyman around the house, but she had seen the things he had done to his house, and he was more than a handyman. He was a true carpenter but without the proper tools. His father told Rose that he was planning to buy his own tools eventually, but he had not done it, so she asked him to help her purchase the right tools. JJ was speechless.

"I do not believe this. When did you buy all of this?" he asked.

"I bought a little here and a little there with your father's help. I hope you like it."

"I love it and especially you."

He kissed Rose like never before, and she knew now what love looked and felt like. The kiss was so intense that they both felt something that needed to be extinguished, but JJ caught himself and stopped. Rose did not want to stop, but she knew she better. What a day and what a night. She could not wait to get back to Mama Mae's and write her family a letter about today. She knew she would not be able to sleep. JJ saw her safely to her front door and gently kissed her goodnight. "I love you, Sunday Rose Tyler, soon-to-be Sunday Rose Gray," he said.

"I love you too, Joe Gray Jr. See you tomorrow?"

"Bright and early."

Chapter 17

They made plans to go to Kittman in February on her birthday to meet Rose's family, tell them she wanted to get married, and make wedding plans if they approved. She was sure they would all love JJ as she did. Rose and JJ had decided on a July wedding. Rose wanted the flowers in bloom in the fields to commemorate her special day. Her new in-laws were all excited about the wedding date, and they could not wait on the event either.

Rose kept asking Mama Mae if she was going to the wedding, and she never gave her a straight answer. Rose had noticed Mama was moving a little slower these days, and she was getting worried about her. One day after coming in from work, she saw Mama in the chair asleep and a piece of paper she had been reading on the floor. Rose picked up the paper and saw that it was from a Doctor Richards's office. The document stated that the recent tests that Mama Mae had taken showed the progression of a growth on her liver.

The doctor outlined some possible treatments that would slow the growth down, but it was not operable. Rose was stunned. She just looked at Mama asleep and suddenly began to cry. Mama woke up and saw Rose standing there and asked her when she had gotten home. Rose tried to gain her composure, but she had to ask Mama about what she had read.

"Mama, I saw this paper on the floor, and it is from a doctor's office. What is this about?"

"Oh, child, it ain't nothin.' This here doctor says I got somethin' on my liver. He wanted to run some more tests, but I said no. Ain't no need in spending money on tests when he can't change nothin.'"

"Mama, do your children know about this?"

"Yeah, I told 'em. That's why they want me to come live with 'em."

"Mama, how long have you known about this growth?"

"Fer a while now."

"Why didn't you tell me about it?"

"Child, why dwell on the bad when so much good is around us? The Lord gonna do what he sees fit when he sees fit. Can't change that."

"What are you going to do?"

"I's thinkin' about moving in with one of my daughters. I haven't quite made up my mind though."

"Mama, I can't believe this. I wanted you to come to my wedding and meet my family." Rose began to cry again.

"I'm still thinkin' on it," Mama replied.

Not able to comprehend what had just happened, Rose ran out of the house and ran to see JJ at the store to tell him about Mama. She saw him outside talking to a customer, and as she got closer, she tried to compose herself. JJ knew something was wrong and asked his father to take care of the customer. Rose ran into JJ's arms and sobbed uncontrollably.

"What is it, Rose?" he asked her.

"JJ, Mama Mae is sick. She has been sick for a while, and she may not be at the wedding. She may be moving in with one of her children."

"How did you find this out?"

"I saw a piece of paper from her doctor. It said she has a growth on her liver. She has known about it for a while but did not tell me. I feel like she is a part of my family. What am I going to do?"

"We are going to pray and ask the Lord to watch over Mama Mae, and if it is in his will, to make her better. We will leave it in his hands."

Rose saw the wisdom in JJ's statement, and she knew he was right. Her mother would say the same thing, and it was basically what Mama had said. They went into the store and told JJ's father, and they all prayed together right there in the store for Mama Mae.

For the next few weeks, Rose saw Mama have good days and not-so-good days. Her good days were still more than her bad days, which she was grateful for. Rose had written to her family and told them about Mama, and her mother said she would put her in her prayers. Again her mother closed her letter with what Rose had known to be true: "God works in mysterious ways. His way is not to question." Rose kept thinking of the time she had met Mama Mae on the bus ride to Dallas. The Lord had put Mama in her path to protect her and keep her safe, and that is what she had done. She'd guided her steps to everything she had experienced in Dallas. "The Lord does certainly work in mysterious ways," Rose muttered to herself.

Chapter 18

As planned, Rose and JJ were on a bus to Kittman, Texas, to meet her family. It was her birthday, but that did not seem important today. She was very happy; Mama Mae had decided to go with them on this trip to meet the family that Rose talked so much about. Rose knew that Mama was not feeling well most of the time, but the last two weeks she'd seemed to be her old self. It was a total surprise when she told Rose she would make the trip to Kittman. During the hour-and-a-half bus ride, Rose talked about her family and the city. She seemed so happy to be going back home and seeing her family. She truly had missed them.

Her brother Jimmie was at the depot waiting for them. Rose hugged her oldest brother and best friend when she saw him. "Jimmie, this is JJ and Mama Mae. They have taken good care of me while I have been in Dallas."

"So this is the man that you are going to marry." Rose was not really surprised to hear these words coming from her brother because he always knew how she felt and thought most times.

"How did you know that, Jimmie? I have not told you we are getting married."

"Rosie, I know you, and I can see it in your face. I never thought I would see you get married to anyone anytime soon, especially before me." Jimmie smiled and hugged his sister again.

"Lord knows it's so good to finally meet this here brother Rose keeps talkin' 'bout," Mama said.

"It is nice to meet you, Jimmie. I can't wait to meet the rest of the family and hear all about growing up with Rose," said JJ.

"Everybody is at home, waiting to meet you and Mama Mae. I have the truck, so JJ, you will have to sit in the back, if you don't mind."

"Not a bit. It will be nice to smell the country air for a change," replied JJ.

"This here seems to be a nice little town. Rose done explained where everyone lives and what they do, so it's like I knowed where I am already."

"Mama, we will be home soon. Are you all right?" asked Rose.

"Yes, child. I's fine. Stop worryin' 'bout me. I'm gon' enjoy myself this weekend and not worry 'bout no pain."

Rose asked Jimmie to drive by the church so JJ and Mama could see where the wedding was going to be. She showed them all of the Tyler land and livestock. As they drove to the front of the house, Rose could see there was a sign over the front door that said, "Welcome home, Sunday Rose, and Happy Birthday." Rose couldn't help but smile. Before the truck had come to a complete stop, the Tyler clan was running out of the door to greet her. Sarah was the first one out of the door, then her brothers. Her father and mother waited on the front porch to greet their oldest daughter, their soon-to-be son-in-law, and the woman that had been a mother to Rose in Dallas.

After first introductions, Rose finally made her way to the front porch and hugged and kissed her parents. "I missed both of you. This is JJ and Mama Mae," she told her parents. They, in turn, greeted both of them as new family friends and invited them inside. The rest of the day, the Tyler family talked about what each of them had been doing since they last saw their daughter and sister.

When Rose finally told her family about the wedding, she was pleasantly surprised when all her mother said was, "When do you need your dress?"

Rose simply replied, "July fifteenth. How did you know?"

"Sunday, I have known you all of your life, and I knew when you mentioned JJ in your letters. It was what you didn't say."

As they ate, the women talked about the wedding plans, the dress that Rose's mother and sister were indeed making, and the guest list. Rose told her mother that JJ's sisters were going to help with the invitations and making the wedding cake. She told her mother that she truly loved JJ and all of his family. Mama Mae told Lottie that Joe Jr. did indeed come from a good Christian family and that she had known his father for many years.

The men, on the other hand, were talking about JJ's business and life on the Tyler farm. After dinner, JJ asked Amos if they could go outside to talk about man things, life on the Tyler farm, and last but not least his approval at marrying his daughter.

The rest of the weekend was a time to get to know JJ and Mama Mae and let her family love them as she did. All things went according to plan. Mama Mae experienced little or no pain over the weekend, and Rose was glad she was able to be involved with the rest of her family. On Saturday night, there was a barbecue at the Johnsons' spread, and JJ was able to see the man that everyone had expected Rose to marry. Rose spoke to her brother's intended, Bernice, and they talked about wedding plans. Bernice was in no rush to get married to Jimmie Lee because they were waiting to save some money. She knew they would eventually get married when they were ready. Bernice was happy for Rose and told her she really liked JJ. The barbecue went on for several hours, and everyone had a good time.

As time drew near for Rose and her Dallas family to leave, she was again dreading the good-byes. After church on Sunday, Rose introduced her fiancé and Mama Mae to Reverend Potter. They discussed the wedding in July and what they wanted on their special day. Reverend Potter was happy to oblige and said they would speak closer to the date. Sarah had prepared a wonderful Sunday meal for everyone.

After the good-byes, Jimmie took his sister and his new acquaintances to the bus depot. The good-byes were hard, but not as hard as the first family good-bye. Another hurdle had been crossed, and Sunday Rose was extremely happy.

Chapter 19

The wedding was drawing nearer each day, and much had happened since her visit home to Kittman to introduce her husband-to-be to her family. She was very happy that Mama Mae had been able to make the trip with her. It was evident that Mama would not be able to attend the wedding ceremony in two weeks, as her illness had progressed in a matter of five months. Mama's oldest daughter, Elsie, had come to Dallas the month before to check on her mother, and Mama had finally decided it was time for her to be near her children and grandchildren in Houston. Rose knew it was for the best, but she couldn't help feeling sad because she was going to miss Mama so much. Rose wished that she could wait at least until after the wedding to leave, but Mama's daughter explained to her that her mother had been instructed by her doctor to check into the hospital in two days to begin a round of treatment. Rose understood, but she was not happy that Mama and her second mother could not be at her wedding.

Rose thought back on the last year of her life and all that had happened to her and all that she'd learned from a woman not even related to her but seemed like a mother and grandmother all in one. Rose knew it was for the best, and she'd known this day was coming, but she hated it.

Mama had already made plans to allow a lady from her church who had no family to live in her house. Mama told the lady, "Jus' take care of my little house. I been happy here." Mama was always helping other people, whatever their circumstances, like Rose. Rose found out later from Mama's daughter that Mama had actually left the house to her if something ever happened to her. She was not looking forward to that, but again, Mama was taking care of her. While Rose was happy that Mama was moving closer to her children, she was also thinking that something could very well happen to Mama in the near future. She didn't want to think about that. This was supposed to be a happy time in a girl's life. She was happy and sad at the same time.

Mama Mae left Dallas, Texas, the Saturday before Rose's wedding. It was a tearful good-bye. "Chile,' I's so happy fer you and JJ. I knowed the moment I see'd you two together what would happen. I knowed you will be happy together. You remember Mama Mae when you start havin' young'uns. I wants to know about married life and how Old Lady Jenkins is takin' care of my house. Rose, you know Mama loves you so much. You make sure you write often, you hear?"

Rose felt like she was losing Mama Mae forever. Deep down in her heart, she knew this would probably be the last time she would see the old lady that had opened her home to a stranger, helped her get a job, and introduced her to her future husband almost a year ago. "Mama, I am going to miss you so much. You make sure you do what the doctors tell you and take your medicine. I will send you pictures of the wedding. I love you, Mama."

Rose didn't try to hold back her tears. Mama was even sniffling every few seconds. As Mama got into her daughter's car, she told JJ to take care of Rose.

"Yes, ma'am, Miss Mae, I will," JJ replied.

The car slowly pulled away from the house that Rose had come to think of as her own with the lady that she had come to love. It seemed that a chapter in Rose's life was closing, but the chapter was filled with so many changes that had made the young girl from Kittman, Texas, a woman in every sense of the word.

Chapter 20

July 15, 1930, was the happiest day of Rose's life. She never knew she could be so happy not singing. She kept thinking about Mama Mae, but her thoughts kept coming back to this special day. JJ and his father had arrived the night before the ceremony, and they had made themselves comfortable in tight living spaces, but no one minded. The other soon-to-be in-laws arrived bright and early the day of the wedding. They came prepared to bake the wedding cake that morning since the ceremony was not until early evening, at 6:15 p.m. Lottie always said it was better to get married when the minute hand was going down and not coming up, whatever that meant.

Jimmie Lee and the rest of the other men-folk took JJ to the Johnson house to change before the ceremony and get out of the women's way. There was a lot of bustling going on, but everything was falling into place. Rose tried on her wedding dress to make sure it fit properly, and of course it did. It was beautiful. Her mother had put lace from her own wedding dress around the hem and neckline, and Sarah had sewn twenty tiny pearl buttons in the back to fasten it.

"If a dress is simple but elegant, that is prettier than a dress with too much color and design," her mother would always say. "Rose, you know when I married your father I was so nervous I wasn't sure I could walk down the aisle. But when I saw that handsome man standing at the altar waiting on me, I forgot about my knees shaking, and all I saw was him. I think you have made a wise choice with JJ, but remember, it is not always going to be like today. There will be tough times on more than one occasion. There will be days when you will wonder if you made the right decision and wonder what would have happened if you had followed another path. But you always remember, if you keep the Lord first in your life and put everything in his hands, you never need to worry."

"Thank you, Mama. I will remember that. I feel like a fairy princess." Rose already knew exactly what her mother was saying to her, but it felt good to hear her mother confirm her belief. She was sure that if she always put the Lord first in everything, she could handle whatever was in store for her and her soon-to-be husband.

Rose's sisters-in-law had completed the three-tier cake, and it was beautiful. The only sad thought Rose allowed herself to have was that Mama Mae could not be there, but she had sent her a letter telling her she was very happy for her and JJ and that she was doing as well as could be expected. She made a point of reminding Rose that she wanted to see the pictures. Rose made sure she had given that important detail to her cousin Herman, who took all of the family pictures at gatherings.

It was still a few hours before the ceremony, and Lottie was making sure everything was as it should be. She was very organized and attended to detail with whatever she touched. She had asked Sister Lorene Allen from the church to be in charge of the food so she wouldn t have anything to worry about there. Sister Lorene was known for her spare ribs and new potatoes, and that is what Lottie asked her to prepare. She was happy to do this for Rose, and she, of course, added a few extras, like her famous broccoli soufflé with mushrooms. Mrs. Rachel Hawkins was in charge of the flowers, and she selected blue gladiolas for the altar and white daisies for the tables in the reception hall. They were the colors that Rose and JJ had selected. The guest list had been kept small, and only fifty people had been invited.

It was time for them to go to the church, and Rose was getting more nervous by the moment. Sarah was going to be her maid of honor. She was only eleven, but she wanted her sister to be a part of her wedding. Rose's brothers would be ushers and help with the reception. Jimmie Lee was in charge of getting the men to the church on time, and Rose was sure he would be timely.

Soon it was 6:00 p.m., and the ceremony was about to begin. Rose and her father were standing in the bride's room, waiting for their time, and Amos took this time to speak to his oldest daughter. "Sunday Rose Tyler, you look so beautiful. This is the last time I can call you Tyler, so I wanted to say it before the ceremony. I am so happy for you and JJ. You have chosen a good man who will take care of you. Let him be the man of the house and you his wife and partner. Remember, your mother and I will always be here if you need us for anything. We have raised a level-headed and smart young woman, and I have no doubts you will have a long and happy marriage."

"Oh, Father, thank you for always being there for me. You and Mother have taught me all I know, and I am so grateful to both of you. I love you so much." Rose paused and got teary-eyed. "Oh no, I can't cry now." At that moment, she heard the music, and without looking at a clock, she knew it was six fifteen on the dot.

The church doors opened, and as Rose and her father stood in the doorway, she spotted JJ at the altar, looking handsome and with a smile on his face she had never seen before. Everyone stood as she walked slowly into the church, holding her father's arm. As her mother had predicted, her nervousness went away as she saw JJ. Sarah had made her way down the aisle, and all eyes were now on Rose. Her walk seemed long down the short aisle, but she finally made it.

Reverend Potter performed the ceremony as he had promised, and at last, Sunday Rose Tyler became Sunday Rose Gray. When she heard Reverend Potter say those words, "Joe, you may now kiss your bride," she knew it had actually happened. She and JJ kissed for the first time as husband and wife, and this kiss was like no other she had experienced with JJ. There was an intensity she had never felt before. *This is what true love feels like,* she thought to herself.

The reception was wonderful, and her mother had made sure everything her daughter had requested had been completed. The food was wonderful, and her new sisters-in-law had created a wonderful wedding cake. She had made the right decision asking them to play this small part in her wedding. This day had been the most wonderful she could ever have imagined. Mr. and Mrs. Joe Gray would now officially become one.

Chapter 21

A few months had passed, and the newlyweds had been very happy. Rose loved taking care of her own household. She loved preparing meals for her new husband and hearing about his day as they ate the dinners that she so carefully cooked each day. Their life seemed to fall into place, as though they had been married for a long time. The newlyweds had their struggles as any other married couple would, such as the lack of money on occasion, but they never seemed to let that get in the way of their happiness. Rose was still happy with her job because it did help pay their bills, and JJ took on more responsibility at the family store to bring home more money for his new family. JJ also had been asked to do more carpentry work at their church, and he was happy to earn the extra money. Rose now knew what it must have been like for her parents trying to raise all of their children when money was scarce. She had learned more from watching her parents deal with everyday life than she realized as well as now really understanding what her father meant by being partners in their marriage.

As promised, Rose sent Mama Mae pictures of her wedding. She had heard from Mama Mae, and she was not getting any worse, which Rose was glad to hear. Her new father-in-law came to dinner often, and Rose was glad to include him in their lives. She had made friends at their new church and was a member of the church choir. While she had not become a singer, she was singing in the church choir, and she was happy. Rose had grown up a lot since her wedding, and she was happy being Mrs. Joe Gray.

Her first Christmas as a married woman had now come. She asked JJ if they could have his family over for Christmas dinner, and, of course, he agreed. They had spent Thanksgiving with her family in Kittman, and she wanted to make sure she spent time with his family as well. She asked her new sisters to help prepare the meal, and they were happy to comply.

It was a lovely dinner and family time. They exchanged gifts and ended the day with a prayer thanking the Lord for their family. After the family left, Rose and JJ exchanged their respective gifts. JJ gave Rose the engagement ring he had promised her all those months ago when he took her to Lena's restaurant on their first date. She was so surprised and so happy that her husband remembered this promise he made to her when he asked her to marry him. JJ was a wonderful and thoughtful husband, she thought to herself. The ring had a small-size diamond with two smaller diamonds on either side, all sitting on a thin gold band that matched her wedding band.

"Thank you, JJ. I love this ring. I never expected anything like this." She kissed him gently and asked him to put the ring on her finger in front of her wedding band. Rose had the same butterflies in her stomach she did the night JJ proposed to her. As she looked at both rings on her hand, she thought to herself that she had never seen anything so beautiful in her life. Rose loved the rings and the thoughtfulness of her husband. "I thought about what I was going to give you, and I was not sure what to buy. After much thought, I decided on three things." She handed him a wrapped box with two pieces of paper and a small book inside. "This is the first one, and I hope you will like it."

He read the first piece of paper, which was a letter from his mother-in-law, Lottie, to Rose. In the letter, Lottie was telling her daughter about a dream she'd had about catfish swimming in clear water.

"I don't understand what this means," he said, perplexed.

"You have to read the second piece of paper," Rose told him. The second piece of paper was a document from a clinic that had the words, "Pregnancy test—positive. Due date in September 1931."

"What does this mean?" JJ asked.

She then handed JJ the small book. The book was titled *Baby Names for Boys and Girls*. JJ looked at Rose and was speechless. "Does this mean what I think it means?"

"What do you think it means?"

"Are we having a baby?"

"That is what the doctor said last week. Are you happy?"

JJ dropped the book and picked up Rose and kissed her passionately. "I am so happy." He kissed her again and yelled at the top of his lungs, "I'm going to be a father!"

Rose had not been sure what JJ would say, and now her worrying was for nothing. This was good news—a new beginning with a new life in the Gray family.

Chapter 22

After JJ had an opportunity to really hear what Rose was telling him, all he could do was grab her and tell her how much he loved her. He kissed her and began to cry. What a Christmas present. He was so happy at the thought of becoming a father. He and Rose had discussed having a baby, but they were just enjoying being Mr. and Mrs. Joe Gray, not trying to have a baby. They talked about the new baby all night.

"I need to know everything the doctor told you," he told Rose. "Is he certain about the due date? I need to make sure I have time to make the baby's cradle. Is this doctor any good? How did you find him? Where will the baby be delivered?"

"JJ, let me answer at least one of your questions before you ask me another one."

"I'm sorry; I am just so happy and excited. Tell me what you know."

"Well, Mabel and Flossie told me about Dr. Smith. I told them I had not been feeling well, and they suspected I might be pregnant, so I wanted to see for myself before I told you. Dr. Smith's office is downtown on Main Street in the Pinkston Clinic. I went to see him last week, and he told me I was indeed pregnant and to the best of his knowledge, the baby would be due the last of September. I am fine, and so is the baby.

"JJ, I know we have not talked about this, but I do not think I want to have the baby in the hospital. I would like to have the baby in Kittman and be delivered by Miss Addie, the midwife who delivered all of us. I trust her, and I feel comfortable with her. She has delivered all of the babies in Kittman, and she is very good. Everybody loves Miss Addie."

"I do not think that is a good idea. I want our baby born in a hospital, delivered by a real doctor. What if something happens? Miss Addie will not have the right equipment or medicine if it is needed. I am sorry, but I cannot agree with this." JJ could not believe what Rose was asking of him.

Though this was one of the happiest moments of both of their lives, the conversation had taken a turn for the worse. This was the first argument they'd had since they had been married. Needless to say, neither of them got any sleep on their first Christmas as a married couple. Rose kept thinking about how she would have her way in the end. After what seemed like an eternity, JJ said, "I would like to speak to Dr. Smith. I need to ask him his opinions on having a midwife deliver our baby. Can we agree to at least do that in a few days?"

Rose was a little angry that JJ had even suggested this because she knew best, but she held her tongue and replied, "Yes, that will be fine. I will call and make the appointment for next week." Even though they had agreed to see Dr. Smith, sleep was still out of the question for either of them.

The next morning, Rose wrote her family as well as Mama Mae and told them her wonderful news. JJ went to see his father to tell him the news. Their good news had been overshadowed by their first argument. They were cordial to each other, but the tension was evident. Rose was sure JJ would come around to her way of thinking in due time. In her letter to her family, she made a point of asking her mother to tell Miss Addie about the baby and to see if she was available in September to help with the delivery. *Why not at least let Miss Addie know in plenty of time?* Rose thought to herself.

As promised, Rose made the appointment with Dr. Smith for a Thursday at noon so she would not miss a full day of work. JJ made sure they arrived at the clinic at eleven thirty, just to be sure. Things were a little better since the conversation at Christmas, but for some reason, JJ thought this visit to see Dr. Smith would change Rose's mind about the baby's delivery.

After greetings and introductions, JJ asked the doctor if Rose and the baby were indeed fine, and the doctor assured him they were. With that response, he was ready with his first and most important question. "Dr. Smith, my wife would like to have the baby delivered by a midwife in Kittman, Texas. Is this safe?"

"Well, there are always risks when babies are not delivered by a certified physician in a sanitary environment with the proper equipment on hand. However, I do know that in many small towns, women rely on midwives to assist in the births of their babies. But if you are asking me if I agree with this form of delivery, I have to say no because of what could go wrong. I am sure there are some good midwives out there, but I would not recommend one to my patients. If, for whatever reason, I had a patient who wanted a midwife, all I could do would be to tell them the risks involved."

Rose heard what the doctor said, but her mind had not changed. She had to ask her own questions at this point. "Doctor, since you do not personally know a midwife, is it possible that some of them could be very good, especially if they have delivered many babies over many years?"

"Yes, Mrs. Gray, that is possible. But my concern is that a midwife has no medical training, and if there is a major complication, they do not have the knowledge and background to make sure the baby and mother are properly cared for."

She looked at JJ, and while he was not saying anything at this point, she knew him well enough to know he was becoming angry at her continued inquiry. However, she still had to ask the doctor one more question. "But Doctor, if the mother has had no complications during her pregnancy, could a midwife deliver the baby with no problems?"

"Again, Mrs. Gray, anything is possible, but I cannot in my professional opinion recommend that any of my patients go to a midwife for their baby's delivery."

At this point, JJ stood up and thanked the doctor for answering their questions. He walked to the door and turned to look at Rose, signaling her to follow him. Rose did not speak another word. Even though the doctor could not recommend midwives delivering babies, she still felt good about what she knew was the right decision.

After much conversation and questions from both JJ and Rose, the two left the doctor's office. At that point all he could say was, "We will talk when we get home this evening." He then kissed Rose good-bye, and they went in separate directions of the city.

Chapter 23

Rose thought about their conversation the rest of the day. She knew JJ was thinking how he could have his way or compromise some way. But how do you compromise on the well-being of the baby, especially this baby? That night, JJ talked and talked and talked, and Rose pretended to listen. She thought maybe she would at least try again to get him to see her point of view. Neither was budging from their way of thinking until Rose asked, "What if I go to Dr. Smith for my monthly checkups and then, when the baby is due, I go to Kittman for the delivery? Of course, I would have to go there maybe a week or so before the due date, but at least I would have been under a doctor's care throughout the whole pregnancy."

She was hoping JJ would go along with this suggestion. JJ quickly agreed with Rose's suggestion, but deep down she was hoping that the closer it got to her delivery date, JJ would come around to her way of thinking. She was sure he would.

Everyone was happy about the news of the baby. Mrs. Goldstein made sure that Rose did not overdo at work, and JJ made sure she did not overdo at home. Mama Mae wrote her to tell her she was happy for her and JJ and that she wanted to make sure Rose sent her a picture of the baby when she was born. Mama knew it was going to be a girl. She never explained how she knew, but she just knew. The correspondence from Mama was becoming less and less. Rose just prayed that Mama Mae's health would allow her to be around for a long time to come, but especially to see a picture of her baby.

Over the next few months, Rose kept her doctor appointments faithfully, and she and the baby progressed nicely, as the doctor always said. It was getting more difficult for her to walk to the bus stop each day, so JJ invested in a used truck, and he began to take Rose to work each day and pick her up. He really wanted her to stop working until after the baby was born because he wanted her to take it easy now that she was carrying his baby, but Rose said that not working was out of the question right now because this was her body and her baby and she knew what was best for both of them. As long as the doctor gave her a clean bill of health, JJ did not force the issue.

There were only two months to go before the baby was due, and Rose, as well as some of the ladies at church, commented that she was gaining a lot of weight. Everyone thought it was because she would be having a large baby. JJ was getting more excited each day. The ladies at church gave Rose a baby shower, and the baby got many handmade blankets, pillows, and clothes. Rose knew her mother and Sarah were making items for the baby as well. She was so surprised and grateful for all of the wonderful gifts she received.

As promised, JJ made the baby a cradle from scratch, and Rose was amazed at how beautiful the cradle was but even more at what beautiful work her husband did on everything he made. "You could make a lot of money from doing carpentry work for people," she would always tell him. But JJ was content just doing it as a hobby or when he was asked to make or repair something for a church member on occasion. Rose was still astonished and proud when she looked at the pulpit each Sunday because JJ had made the entire pulpit where Reverend Jacobs stood each Sunday to deliver his message, as well as the podium he used to hold the Word of God. Reverend Jacobs always made a point of thanking JJ for his hard work in the church. That was probably why JJ got the amount of business he did from his church friends. *Oh, how he could do such great things with his ability, if he only would do it,* Rose often thought to herself.

The last month before the delivery was approaching, and JJ insisted that Rose stop working. She agreed. Mrs. Goldstein understood and made sure Rose knew her job would be waiting after the baby was born.

It was now the first week of September, and Rose had weekly doctor appointments. JJ made sure he made every appointment with her. He wanted to make sure she and the baby were doing fine.

The doctor saw no problems with the baby or the delivery. He guessed the baby would be born between September 18th and 25th. "The baby is progressing nicely," the doctor said, his usual diagnosis. However, on this particular visit, he asked a question that he had never broached before. "Is there any history of twins in your family, Mrs. Gray?"

"Well, my mother had twins, but one died in childbirth. It was a boy. Why did you ask that, Dr. Smith?"

"Well, it appears I am now hearing two heartbeats. The second baby was hiding behind its sibling, and I could not hear the heartbeat."

Rose could not speak. This would explain all of the extra weight she was gaining. How was she going to manage with two babies? The first person she wanted to tell the news was her mother. She hated to admit it, but she was afraid at the thought of having twins. However, she knew her mother would understand her fear since she had been pregnant with twins.

JJ was astounded to hear this news. "Doctor, is everything okay with Rose and the babies?"

"Yes, all seems to be fine. I want you to take it easy and get a lot of rest each day. You may go into labor before the eighteenth because of the two babies, so be prepared."

Rose looked at JJ's face, and she noticed a smile as well as a look of relief. She was sure he was thinking that now she would agree to have the babies delivered by Dr. Smith.

On the way home, Rose asked JJ what names he thought they should consider now that they were having twins. If a boy, they had decided on Joseph Amos after JJ, his father, and her father. If it was a girl, they thought of Geraldine Mae after JJ's mother and Mama Mae. Now that they were having two babies, they would simply use both sets of names. It was easy. Rose already knew it would be a boy and a girl, and she would not even entertain the idea of two boys or two girls.

After they arrived home, JJ started right on the second cradle. Rose rested, but before she took her daily nap, she wrote her mother a letter to let her know the latest good news and to make sure that Miss Addie knew about the twins so she would be prepared. She told her she would be in Kittman the next week. She wasn't sure when exactly the babies would be born, but she wanted to arrive before the possible due date, given what Dr. Smith had told them today. With that taken care of, she slept peacefully, as best as she could now.

At dinner that night, JJ made sure that Rose did nothing but enjoy her meal. He prepared the entire meal while Rose slept, and she remembered why she had fallen in love with him. He was so thoughtful and kind. "JJ, you do know I love you dearly, don't you?"

"I know I love you with all of my heart. I love my babies even before they are born because you are having them."

"JJ, I still want to go to Kittman to have our babies. I know you do not want me to do this, but I must. It will make me feel more comfortable, and I am certain everything will be all right. Please trust me to make sure our babies' deliveries are happy for me."

All JJ could do was listen. Not saying a word, he got up from the table, left their home, and drove off. Rose could not understand why JJ did not see her point of view on this.

Later that night, JJ arrived back home, and when he entered their home, all he could say was, "I do not agree with you on this, but I will not fight you on it either. You know how I feel and my wishes. If you choose to go to Kittman and have Miss Addie deliver our babies, I will drive you there myself. I only pray nothing goes wrong, because if it does, I will never be able to forgive you." JJ left the room and continued work on the second cradle. For whatever reason, Rose was confident about her decision, and she wanted to show her husband she knew her decision was the right one.

For the next few days, JJ was cordial with Rose, and she with him, but it was not the same household that had seen laughter and unending conversation only a month before. Rose prepared to leave Dallas in two days to go to Kittman and become a mother. She made sure everything in her Dallas home was in its proper place and ready for the two new lives. JJ had, as usual, done a wonderful job with the second cradle. The babies' area of their bedroom was in order, and there were two of all items ready for little Joseph and Geraldine. Rose had decided they would probably call the babies Amos and Mae. She made this decision all on her own as well. No surprise there.

Chapter 24

The trip to Kittman was uneventful and mostly quiet. JJ did as he'd told Rose he would do—drive them to Kittman and stay with her until and during the delivery, no questions asked. When they arrived at Rose's parents' home, her family was waiting to greet her and JJ. They all commented about how big she was and how glad they were to see both of them. Miss Addie was there as well, and Rose hugged her for what seemed like a full minute. She was so glad to see her. She knew there was nothing to worry about. She introduced her to JJ, and he replied with, "Hello, nice to finally meet the woman who will deliver my babies." Everyone felt the tension in his voice, but no one commented about it.

Conversations continued throughout the day about family and the births of new family members. JJ was noticeably quiet during the rest of the day and finally just decided to take a walk alone to clear his head. Rose's father took this opportunity to ask Rose to walk with him to the barn. Once outside, Amos had to ask, "Is everything okay with you and the babies, and is everything all right with you and JJ? I noticed you were both awfully quiet."

"Yes, Father, the babies are fine, but JJ is not happy because he did not want the babies delivered by Miss Addie. He thinks that when the time comes, the delivery will not be okay. He has nothing against Miss Addie, but he wanted me to go to a clinic and let a real doctor help with the deliveries. I tried to tell him that we all trust Miss Addie even though she is not a real doctor."

Rose's father listened as his daughter continued to explain JJ's fears. "Rose, you have to pray about this as you do with everything and leave it with the Lord," her father told her. "The Lord will take care of you and the babies how he sees fit."

Rose listened to her father intently and agreed to leave it with the Lord. In order to relieve some of the tension about the babies' deliveries, Amos told Rose that he was going to ask JJ to look at the cabinets in the kitchen for her mother. Lottie had always wanted some new cabinets with more space, but her father kept putting it off. "Now that my son-in-law is here, I will pass this request on to him." Amos smiled.

"JJ will be happy to help Mother. This will keep his mind off other things," Rose responded, hoping that it would.

For the next few days, Rose rested, and JJ occupied his time with the kitchen cabinets. Miss Addie made a point of coming by each day to check on her patient.

She felt Rose's stomach to see what positions the babies had moved into. She could tell just by mashing on her stomach what position the babies were in and what body parts she was feeling at that moment. "Looks like these here babies is almost ready to be born. May be here by the end of the week."

Rose was ready for "b-day," as her brother Jimmie called it. He teased her often about how large she was as well as other brother-and-sister barbs. She had missed talking to her best friend. She asked him when he and Beatrice would be finally tying the knot.

He explained to Rose that maybe by the end of the year, they would be ready. Rose was happy to hear that he almost had all of the money to purchase the Garrett farm and had put a down payment on it so Mrs. Garrett would not sell it. Their father always told his children to treat business, when money was involved, like business, and that was what her brother was doing. Rose could tell he was happy, as were her other brothers and sister.

She and Sarah had visited a lot since she had been home. Rose could see Sarah had grown up quite a bit in the last few months, but she could also see some of her bouts of illness had taken a toll on her walking. But Sarah did not let that get her down.

Chapter 25

If Miss Addie was right, Rose and JJ would be proud parents in two to three days. In bed, JJ felt compelled to tell Rose how he felt one more time. "Rose, I love you so much. I would die if anything happened to you or the babies. I know I have been difficult to live with these last few days, but I am just worried. Don't blame me for caring and loving you and our babies." He kissed her gently, and she cried softly.

All she could muster to say was, "I love you too, so much. Thank you for loving me." With that, they fell off to sleep, and for the only time in at least two months, both she and her husband had a good night's sleep.

For the next two days, Rose was very uncomfortable. No position made her feel better. Miss Addie decided to stay at the house until the babies were born. JJ was glad at that. No one in the house had slept the last two days, what with the impending births. They all felt Rose's discomfort and tried to make her as comfortable as possible.

On the third night, when all was quiet, Rose let out a scream, and Miss Addie sprung into action. She asked Lottie to boil some water and get plenty of clean towels, rags, and sheets. She asked the men to leave the house and told them to expect a long night. Lottie tried to comfort her daughter as much as she could. It was evident Miss Addie had done this many times. She did not hesitate telling Rose when to push and when to breathe and when to rest. "Lottie, girl, this is gonna be a long night," she said.

After twenty-four hours of labor, time was coming near. Miss Addie told Rose to push hard so she could see her new babies. Rose did the best she could do and yelled at the top of her lungs, and one baby was in the world. Miss Addie looked at the baby boy, and she noticed right away that he was not moving. She spanked the baby's behind, but there was still no sound of life or movement. Miss Addie was at a loss at what had happened. Rose's first baby had come into this world but would never know his parents, his grandparents, or his younger sibling.

Lottie took the baby from Addie, and she saw the baby boy was a bluish color and lifeless. She could not say a word to comfort her daughter. Miss Addie focused her attention back to Rose and the second baby that was waiting to come into the world.

Rose let out another yell, and she tried to push, but something was wrong. This baby did not come out, and Miss Addie thought maybe the cord was wrapped around the baby's neck. She tried and tried to help the baby, but it was taking longer and longer.

"Lottie, I cain't budge this here baby. There is a big problem up there. I want you to get behind Rose and push on her belly to try and push the baby out." Lottie complied, and after about forty-five minutes of doing this, the baby still was no closer to being born.

All Rose could think of was JJ and that what he had felt and thought all along had come to pass. She cried and asked to see her dead son, but before her mother could bring the baby into her view, Rose felt another surge of pain, and she felt like she had to push again. *Oh no*, Rose thought to herself. *What if the second baby does not make it either?* Rose's only thought was what JJ would say and do. He still had not been told about his son. "Lord, please let this baby be born alive and healthy," Rose said out loud. The pain came and went for the next thirty minutes, and Rose was getting more tired and more anxious to see her baby born.

Chapter 26

In between pains and Miss Addie saying, "I needs you to push, Rosie girl," Rose's thoughts kept going back to her dead baby boy and how she would tell her husband that his son, whom he had never seen, was dead. The next pain felt different than the rest of what she had been experiencing, and fear suddenly crept through Rose's sheer being. She began to cry uncontrollably.

"Rose, I cain't do this here birthin' by myself; I needs you to help with this," Miss Addie said. Rose could not and did not want to push because she knew she could not face another dead baby and the hatred of her husband. "Keep pushin,' baby girl. I kin' see the head. Oh my Lord, chile,' I see'd this here baby comin,'" Miss Addie said loudly.

Rose let out a desperate yell and remarked, "Lord, be with my baby now. Let it be alive." At that moment, Rose felt like she had when her son had finally come into the world. She knew what that meant, and she could not bear it if this baby was born dead.

Lottie was crying along with her daughter. Even though Lottie knew that her daughter was a strong woman, she was sure she would not be able to handle the deaths of two babies in the same day. "Lord, help this baby," she cried. As Lottie closed her eyes to pray silently, Miss Addie yelled, "Lordy, I see'd it, but it ain't movin' no more. Lottie, I thinks you bes' go git the husband." Lottie looked at her daughter, and Rose's expression told her to wait a little longer before she went to get her son-in-law.

At that moment she heard a loud knock on the door. "Am I a father yet?" JJ asked.

"I will be out in a second, JJ," Lottie answered. Not knowing what to say to him, she looked at her daughter for words to say, but Rose simply stared into space.

At that moment, Rose let out a loud scream, and JJ replied, "I think I better wait a little longer." Lottie silently thanked the Lord for intervening at this moment.

"It hurts so bad, Miss Addie. Please help me," Rose said.

"Push, chile'; you got to do some work here. I see'd this here baby's head. Looks like things is gettin' ready to happen now. I guess the Lord jes' wanted to let you rest fer a while. He knows best. Push, little mama, push," Addie kept saying.

Rose let out a loud and long yell, and at the end of this yell, a baby girl was born. Miss Addie spanked the baby's behind, and the first baby cry was heard by all. Rose let out tears of joy because she had a baby daughter. She was not only crying tears of joy but tears of sadness as well.

"Is my baby girl all right, Miss Addie? Please say she is all right," Rose asked.

"I do believes this here is a healthy baby girl, Rosie. She kinda looks like you looked when I brung you into this here world. She gots a head full of jet-black hair, and she already filled out. You knowed I tried to saves the baby boy, but he had a problem in your belly, and I could not fix it. Baby girl, I am so sorry."

"I know, Miss Addie. Thank you for all of your help."

All Rose could think of was JJ and how what he felt all along had come to light. She cried and asked to see her daughter. While she looked at her baby girl and thanked the Lord for sparing one of her babies, Lottie went to get JJ. When he arrived in the room and saw Rose holding one baby and not two, he knew what had happened. He walked slowly toward Rose and his one baby, and he slowly began to cry for the baby in Rose's arms and the baby he eyed wrapped in a towel on a lonely bed.

"What happened?" he asked.

"Miss Addie said that something was wrong with our son and she could not save him."

Both JJ and Rose cried and hugged each other.

JJ could feel the rage rising, and he had to say his piece and what was on his mind. "This is what I said would happen, and you would not listen to me. I wanted our babies born in a clinic just in case something like this happened. You did not even give our baby a chance to live." With that, JJ left the room and the house without a word to anyone. Rose was crying at her husband's words, but she could not say a word in her defense. Lottie tried her best to comfort Rose, but she could only think about JJ and his last words to her.

Everyone understood her pain and JJ's reaction. Now, not only did they have to celebrate the birth of a daughter and granddaughter, but they had to plan a funeral for a son and grandson.

JJ finally came back to the house late into the night. Rose was in bed waiting for him. When he walked into the room, all he could say was, "Is my daughter okay?"

"Yes, she is fine."

"How do you know?"

"Miss Addie gave her a clean bill of health."

Rose knew after she said these words and by the expression on JJ's face that he held his tongue and did not say what he really wanted to say, and she was glad. "Rose, I don't think I will ever get over the death of my son when it could have been different. I begged you to go to Dr. Smith and the clinic for the deliveries, but you knew better. I may never be able to forgive you for this.

"You know, I never told you this, but your father and I had a talk before we got married. I wanted to formally ask him for your hand in marriage. At that time, your father told me he approved of our marriage, but he had to tell me some things about you. First, he said that you were a good girl, but you were headstrong, very opinionated, and that sometimes you could be difficult if it was something you did not want to do. He

A New Beginning and a New Life

told me to always remember that after we got married I would be the husband and head of the household but that you would question my decisions and sometimes tell me there was a better way. I knew when he said these words that it would take every ounce of patience I could muster to reason with or go against you, and now I see what he was saying to me. So now that your father's words have come true at the expense of my son, tell me, Rose, what do I tell my family? Where will the funeral be? Do you expect my family to drive down here to attend a funeral when they were expecting for us to come back with two babies? What have you decided for us to do about this?"

Rose was speechless. How could JJ bring her father's words into this argument? She began crying uncontrollably and could not even look at JJ, let alone answer his questions. She knew things had changed for them, but how would she ask her husband to take charge of a baby's funeral when it did not have to be this way? Still crying, Rose could not respond to any of JJ's questions. He had some valid points and questions that needed answers, and she finally chose her responses carefully.

"JJ, I know you did not want Miss Addie to deliver our babies, and I was wrong for that. I am sorry that our son didn't make it, and his death will haunt me for the rest of my life. I know it is going to take you some time to forgive me, but please, I am begging you not to give up on us and me. I do love you and our daughter so much. Please do not leave me and our family."

JJ did not speak a word. He walked over to his baby daughter in Rose's arms and gently picked her up, kissed her small forehead, and took her to another room so he could be with his daughter alone.

Rose knew that her actions had caused an irreparable rift between them, and it was her fault. How had her perfect life come to this moment?

Sunday Rose Tyler Gray said a silent prayer asking the Lord for forgiveness and the words to speak to her husband. After her prayer, no words came, and she felt more alone by the minute.

Only time, prayer, and faith could heal the pain and hopefully bring her husband and his love back to her. Rose knew that it would take some time, but she was sure her husband would forgive her. If it was the last thing she did, she would make this happen. Now, she and her husband had to think about burying their baby son. She was hoping that they would help each other get through this painful time and hopefully be a happy family.

www.ingramcontent.com/pod-product-compliance
Lightning Source LLC
Chambersburg PA
CBHW052055070526
44584CB00017B/2184